First Steps in
Global Music

Karen Howard

GIA PUBLICATIONS, INC. • CHICAGO

Acknowledgments

A book as diverse as this required the help of many generous and talented people. For help with languages, thank you to Bisrat Bayou, Dr. Olga Herrera, Salam Murtada, Maia Kachkachishvili, Juliana Cantarelli Vita, Joko Sutrisno, and Ali Rana.

For beautiful repertoire, my sincere thanks to Dr. Kedmon Mapana, Dr. Jean Kidula, and Rachel Hickman.

Continuing appreciation to Dr. Christopher Roberts for listening to all of the songs as they were collected and offering thoughtful feedback.

Many thanks to Adrienne Gaylord for the incredible instrument drawings (and RG) and to Sophia Gaylord for singing on the recordings and demonstrating the movements. I am so glad we are all on the same team.

A special and continuing thank you to Dr. Patricia Shehan Campbell for the inspiration to wonder about people, music, and cultures throughout my career.

First Steps in Global Music
Karen Howard

G-9966
ISBN: 978-1-62277-399-2

www.giamusic.com

Table of Contents

Foreword by John M. Feierabend

Here is a book like no other.

While *First Steps in Music* has always promoted teaching the folk music of the USA in all its diversity, this book completes a long-planned enhancement to that curriculum by providing authentic global repertoire with curriculum-relevant songs.

Dr. Karen Howard's expertise as a teacher of First Steps in Music and as an authority on global music is unique and brings profound insights to this publication. Here, teachers will find highly useful songs and activities for the elementary classroom while gaining valuable knowledge of the cultural context, people, and places from where these songs played important roles.

In addition, Dr. Howard has accompanied this book with much-needed recordings to facilitate learning both proper pronunciations and authentic style—a music teacher's dream.

I am sure you will find this collection vital to your teaching and deeply enriching for your students.

Introduction

This book is intended to support music educators in diversifying their song collections while also offering insights into the cultures from which the songs, chants, and games originated. The repertoire was selected based on tunes, stories, and games that have captured the musical and playful imagination and participation of children. Also considered were accessibility for teachers and children in teaching and learning settings. You are encouraged to add more to this collection. Let one tune inspire you to learn more of a culture, or to steer you toward a culture that suits your interests, or your school community, or a community that you feel is underrepresented in your music curriculum. Enjoy the newness of some of the languages and the familiar nature of some of the games, and add your own and your students' creative touches to elevate the musical experiences.

Authenticity and Context

You may feel overwhelmed at the thought of mastering songs from so many cultures with worry of being "authentic." Many music teachers have trained predominantly, or even exclusively, in Western European traditions. The point here is not to expect instant expertise in all of the music cultures included in this book. The carefully selected songs are meant to offer informed choices that can be incorporated into existing curricula in meaningful ways.

Our understanding of authenticity has grown over the decades. We know that the culture of your classroom is important to consider along with the culture of the music brought to the children. Songs do not stay frozen as though they are on display in a museum. Songs are reborn with each performance, each setting, each group of children, and each hybrid as the song meets technology and travels back and forth between cultural influences. Consider the sea shanty: long at home on a ship with sailors, these tunes have become standards in the elementary music classroom. Even murder ballads, centuries-old tales of betrayal and deceit, have found their way into lullabies and storybooks. Perhaps with time, a more diverse repertoire will be considered standard in the elementary music classroom, eliminating the need for the category of "world" or "global" music.

Performance Style

The materials gathered in this book include folk songs and chants performed over generations. The notation is not meant to serve as an absolute, but rather it is intended to present a version for your consideration as the teacher. Sometimes we feel obligated to perform a song because it is notated in a certain way. Keep in mind that notation is akin to taking a picture—it captures a moment, but it does not represent the whole when it comes to folk music, which is alive and ever evolving. Change the key to one that suits your students, or you. Listen to recorded versions by different groups and artists, and then incorporate those variations into your version. Free yourself from singing precisely what you see on the page and allow vocal stylings to enter your performance. Avoid designing a lesson with notation reading as your primary goal with these particular songs, as it often dictates the way a song is sung—"If I want students to read this, then I have to sing it in a way they can read." This is rarely if ever the way these songs are sung. There are many things you can return to in this material to use for notation purposes, but put the artistry and musicality first. Then, you can see what remains for notation purposes.

Teaching Unfamiliar Languages

This book contains songs in English and 16 other languages. The expectation is not that you become fluent in these languages. It is certainly possible to learn the basic phonetic rules for one song at a time, one language at a time. This does become easier the more often you try it. The songs become less intimidating when you build up your skill level at grappling with pronouncing different sounds. For all of the songs included in this book, I practiced the pronunciations extensively. I always have the lyrics handy, and I often rely on the phonetic spelling. It is common to feel like you have mastered a song, as there are so many opportunities to repeat it. Yet when you go back to the song the next year, it may seem as though you have never seen the song and the syllables feel difficult on your tongue. You will find, though, that the re-acquaintance period shortens with each revisit to the piece and the culture. Little by little, your comfort with the different music cultures and languages will grow, as will your students' enjoyment and comfort. As David Mallet's beloved folk song says, "Inch by inch, row by row, gonna make this garden grow."

You may notice inconsistencies with spellings that you see in other sources. Many of the languages represented in this book are transliterated—meaning they were changed from one alphabet into another (such as Japanese kahnji or Bulgarian in the Cyrillic alphabet). There are some standard interpretations to be found, but even more common are multiple accepted ways to transliterate particular words. As not all music teachers are familiar with IPA (International Phonetic Alphabet), I opted to use phonetic spellings for pronunciation assistance throughout. These are meant to be paired with the recordings, as any sort of written representation of a spoken sound will be limited.

Children's Music Culture: What We Know

When attempting to cover global music in one short book, only a few select music cultures can make their way into the final product. By no means an exhaustive resource, but rather a starting point, this book is intended to set a tone for working with songs from a broad range of cultures and traditions. While no two cultures are the same, there are certainly some shared music-making activities and song types that can be commonly found in relation to certain occasions, including but not limited to funerals, births, harvest, weather, medicinal, related to animals, lullabies, education, dedicated to an individual, competitions, nonsense, battle stories, work tales, traveling, prayer, greeting, and farewell.

Resources

The book is organized by geographical region. At the end of each geographical region is a listing of websites, recordings, books, and online videos that are of good quality and include contextual information. The more information, the more reliable the source! These are not meant to be exhaustive lists. Take a look, have a listen, read some pages, and see what captures your attention, and what might capture your students' imaginations. Some lists are longer than others, and this simply represents the extent of my personal research on the particular culture, not the overall availability or quantity.

In addition, included at the back of the book is an alphabetical index of all songs included in this book, as well as an index that organizes the songs based on First Steps activity categories (fragment singing, simple songs, movement for form and expression, movement with the beat, and songtales).

The Recordings

There are two recordings for each of the songs and chants that are in languages other than English: the first is spoken pronunciation, and for the songs, the second is a simple presentation of the tune. These recordings are intended to assist you in your own practice. Let the recordings support you so you can feel confident in singing the songs by yourself for the children.

I also intentionally did not arrange or accompany the songs. As folk material, the possibilities are wide open. Do not consider these songs frozen in any particular format. Find a key that works for you and the children, a setting that feels comfortable. If you add an accompaniment, make it one that you feel good about and that considers both the original context and your classroom context. If you accompany with an instrument or groove or styling not typically found in the culture, no problem! Simply be sure to talk to the children about creativity and your hybrid performance, and then take the time to let them hear the original sound source.

The Collection

The songs included in this book were selected with the following First Steps workout activity categories in mind:

Fragment Singing

> Allo, Monsieur (Canada)
> Kavuli Tutu (Kenya) – Call and Response
> Maludeje (Tanzania)
> Marobo (Kenya) – Call and Response
> Mbukwenyi (Tanzania)
> Ó Emboleé (Brazil)
> Pico y Pala (Cuba)
> Tarnegol (Israel)
> Yave Nguva Yezhizha (Zimbabwe)

Simple Songs

> Arroro (Guatemala)
> Eshuru (Ethiopia)
> Here Comes Doctor Riding (Jamaica)
> Iavnana (Georgia)
> Kirisu (Japan)
> Rain, Rain (Ghana)
> Sutartinės (Lithuania)
> Taoto (Tahiti)

Movement for Form and Expression

> Cradle Song (Japan)
> El Coqui (Puerto Rico)
> Ó Emboleé (Brazil)
> Po Atarau (New Zealand)
> Trois Canards (Canada)

Movement with the Beat

Ache Kuwwa (Pakistan)
Caballo Blanco (Chile)
Dobry Wieczór Wam (Poland)
Ferrocarril (Peru)
Here Comes Doctor Riding (Jamaica)
Lollipop (Jamaica)
Maludeje (Tanzania)
Mbukwenyi (Tanzania)
Mo Li Hua (China)
O Anane Kéké (Indonesia)
Ó Emboleé (Brazil)
Pin Pin Jarabín (Mexico)
Po Atarau (New Zealand)
Tic Tic Tic Ya'um Sleiman (Lebanon)
Toi Si Bonne (Haiti)
Yave Nguva Yezhizha (Zimbabwe)

Songtales

Click Go the Shears (Australia)
Mo Li Hua (China)
Moe Muničko Kokiče (Bulgaria)
Pico y Pala (Cuba)
Poreho (Tahiti)
Tic Tic Tic Ya'um Sleiman (Lebanon)

MUSIC FROM
Africa

Africa

omprised of more than 50 countries, the continent of Africa is often described in music books as one location rather than attending to the diversity within each region, and then again within each country. Take the time to know which country a song is from, as well as the language, the translation, and the context in which the song is performed. Generally, we do not find a song listed as "European Folk Song," but it is quite common to see "African Folk Song." A change in this habit is overdue. It is easier than ever to find sociohistorical and sociocultural information about music. This book models an approach to recognizing the unique features of each music culture as we travel through the songs and chants.

West Africa

West Africa includes the following countries:

Benin	Ghana	Liberia	Nigeria
Burkina Faso	Guinea	Mali	Senegal
Cape Verde	Guinea-Bissau	Mauritania	Sierra Leone
Gambia	Ivory Coast	Niger	Togo

Music in **Ghana**

Ghana has a wide variety of traditional and contemporary music genres. For contemporary music, Highlife is the most dominant style and has spread throughout West Africa. Highlife's popularity led to it being considered the national music during the era of independence in the 1950s. Ghana was the first colonized country in Africa to gain independence under the leadership of President Kwame Nkruma in 1957.

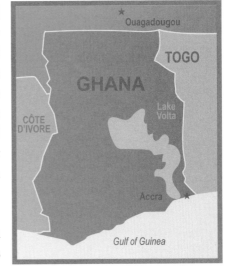

There is a strong tradition of indigenous music in Ghana's rural areas, and it filters into the sounds of urban music. Traditional music genres include court music for chiefs, ceremonial music for special occasions, work songs for harvest and home chores, and recreation. Some genres have large drum ensembles or horn groups; others have *balafon* (large xylophones with gourd resonators) or an assortment of bells, such as *gankogui, tokee,* and *firikiwa*; and other areas use mostly fiddles, *donno* (talking drum) ensembles, and even lutes. The names of the instruments change between ethnic groups and languages, but the shapes and sounds are similar.

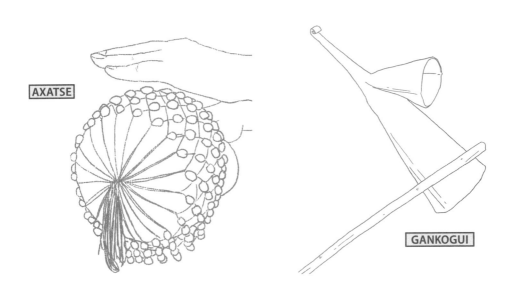

AXATSE

GANKOGUI

TOKEE

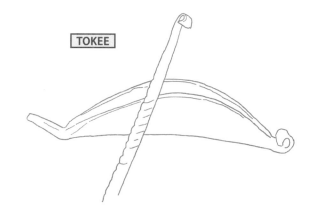

KPANLOGO DRUM

FIRIKIWA

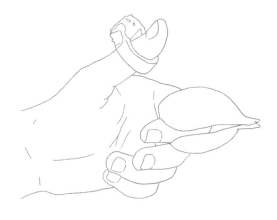

DONNO

BALAFON

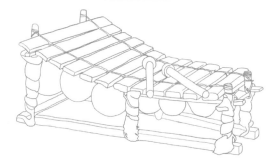

Rain, Rain

Simple Songs

Rain, rain, go a - way. Go and come a -

no - ther day, Go and come a - no - ther day.

Lit - tle chil - dren want to play.

Lit - tle chil - dren want to play.

Lyrics
Rain, rain, go away.
Go and come another day,
Go and come another day.
Little children want to play.
Little children want to play.

Teaching Considerations
- The preschool and kindergarten children who taught me this song wiggled their hips back and forth, hands on hips, to the beat on "Little children want to play."
- Perform solos on each line.
- Extend the form so A = singing and B = playing the rhythm of the song on an un pitched percussion instrument (e.g., hand drum, wood block, claves, rhythm sticks).
- If your students are working with these rhythms:
  - Create flashcards to play with the measures.
  - Transfer particular rhythms to instruments (e.g., eighth notes on wood block, quarter notes on hand drum with mallet).

East Africa

East Africa includes the following countries:

Burundi	Mozambique
Comoros	Rwanda
Djibouti	Seychelles
Eritrea	Somalia
Ethiopia	South Sudan
Kenya	Sudan
Madagascar	Tanzania
Malawi	Uganda
Mauritius	

Music in Ethiopia

Ethiopia has been on the mend after many years of civil war. Long periods of struggle (such as during a war) can profoundly impact the survival of artistic practices and children's recreational music making. A long-standing curfew during the war era put a stop to evening concerts and music making together for multiple generations. Musicians are combing through older recordings and bringing traditions back to their communities.

The most commonly spoken language is Amharic from the Amhara people, one of the world's oldest Christian communities. Traditional music is found at the core of most styles in modern-day Ethiopia. Many musicians are well versed in older, traditional genres as well as contemporary genres and move seamlessly between creating interesting hybrids of old and new.

A popular scale is a five-note pentatonic mode with large intervals between the pitches, which results in an unresolved feeling. This is often paired with characteristic asymmetrical rhythm patterns. Traditional instruments include the *krar* (lyre), *masenqo* (one-string fiddle), *washint* (flute), and *kebero* (percussion). Brass bands are popular, and pop and rock band instrumentations are also readily found.

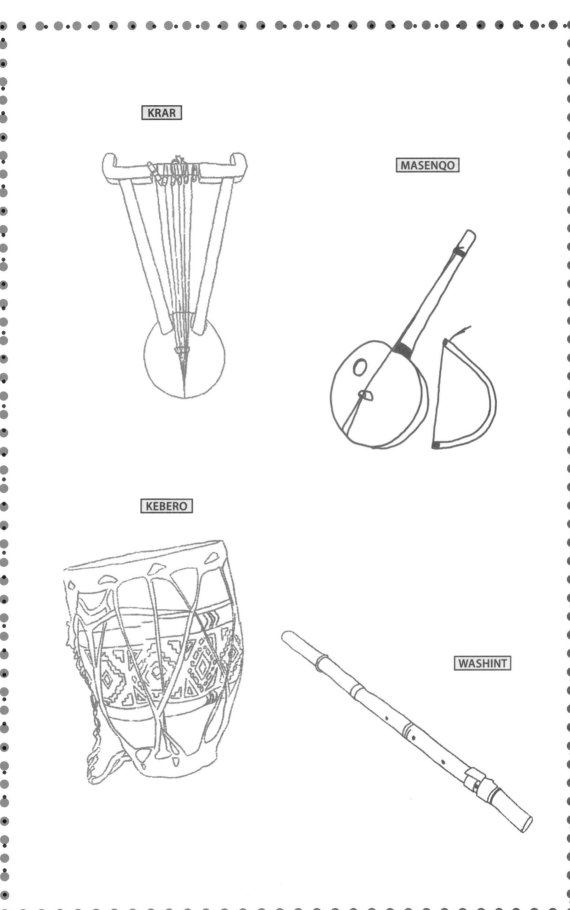

KRAR

MASENQO

KEBERO

WASHINT

Eshururu

Simple Songs

E - shu - ru - - - - ru - ru

E - shu - ru - ru - ru

Ye - ma - mu - ye _ i - na - tih

to - lo - neh_____ yih - let - ih

Weh - te - tu - nih be - gu - ya

da - bo - wu - nih beh hee ya

yih - ze - shi_____ le - te

E - shu - ru

Amharic	English
Eshurururu (2x)	Hush, hush, hush, hush
Eh-shoo-roo-roo-roo	
Yemamu ye inatih toloneh yihletih	Mommy will come back soon
yeh mah-moo yeh eh-naht toh-loh neh yih-leht(ih)	
Wehtetunih beguya	on the back of a donkey
Weh-te-toon(ih) beh-goo-yuh	
dabowunih beh hee ya yihzeshilete	with bread and milk in her arms
dah-boh-woon(ih) beh-ee-yah yih-zeh-shih-leht(ih)	

Contextual Considerations

I had help with this song from two undergraduate students, Rachel Hickman and Bisrat Bayou. Rachel introduced me to the lullaby in diction class. Bisrat assisted me with the pronunciation. Bisrat's parents moved to the United States during the war, and he was born shortly after their arrival. He remembers his mother singing him this very tune during his younger years. When I asked him about the many variations I found and heard, he acknowledged that there are many variations of the tune, with the end goal always being a relaxed baby or child.

Teaching Considerations

- Flip all "r" consonants lightly.
- Deemphasize "ih" and do not give this sound much phonation time.

Music in **Kenya**

There are more than 40 ethnic groups in Kenya with the larger groups including:

Akamba	Luhya	Maasia
Bajuni	Luo	Turkana
Borana		

Each of Kenya's major language groups has its own musical style. It is different in the cities where a mix of languages, genres, and eras can be heard in clubs, on the radio, and in videos. As is common in so many cultures, what is sometimes referred to as "local language music" (often called "folk music") is trying to survive amidst imported sounds from the internet. Guitars are popular with locally influenced tunings and playing styles. Other traditional instruments include various drums, *kalimbas* (thumb pianos), the *nyatiti* (lyre), the *obokano* (larger lyre), and the *chamonge* guitar (a cooking pot strung with wires).

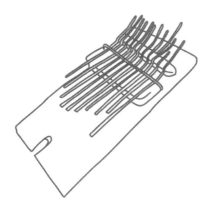

KALIMBA

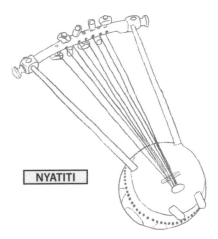

NYATITI

Kavuli Tutu

Fragment Singing – Call and Response

Ka - vu - li (tu - tu), Ngwa - tie

mwa - na (tu - tu), Ndu - la - ne - ne - the (tu -

tu), Mbe - mbai - ki - wa (tu - tu), No - syo tu -

ka - ya (tu - tu) No - syo tu - ka - ya, (tu -

tu) No - syo tu - ka - ya (tu - tu). Ka - vu

Kikamba	English
Kavuli (tutu) *kah-voo-lee (too-too)*	Dove,
Ngwatie mwana (tutu) *(n)gwah-teem wah-nah*	Hold my baby for me
Ndulane nethe (tutu) *(n)doo-lah-neh neh-(d)eh*	so that I may dance with its father
Mbembaikiwa (tutu) *(m)behm-bah ee-kee-wah*	while the corn is ripening.
Nosyo tukaya (tutu) (3x) *Noh-syoh too-kah-yah*	That is what we shall eat.

Contextual Considerations

- This tune is in *Kikamba*, one of many languages in the larger Bantu family.
- *Ki* means language, and *Kamba* is an ethnic group in Kenya living predominantly in the Eastern Province.
- *Kavuli Tutu* is a song for children to sing when it is time to welcome the ripening of the corn. Corn is one of the main food staples for Kamba families living in rural areas, along with beans, peas, and mixed greens. These are crops that can grow during a rainy season.

Teaching Considerations

- Common letter clusters include "mb," "nd," and "ng" and begin with a closed "m" (lips closed) or closed "n" (no vowel added after).
- In this particular song, the "m" and "n" do not phonate. Rather, the closed letter is shaped before sounding the next letter. Use the recordings to catch the nuance of this pronunciation.

Marobo

Fragment Singing – Call and Response

Luo

(Call) Marobo
Mah-roh-boh

(Response) Tandarobo
Tahn-da-roh-boh

(All) Nyitindo matindo biuru watugi
Nyee-teen-doh mah-teen-doh bee-oo-ree wah-too-gee

koda kidi watugi koda kidi
koh-dah kee-dee wah-too-gee koh-dah kee-dee

Luhya

Mgeni yatsa na a salitsa
(M)geh-nee yah-tsah nah sah-lee-tsah

English *(general)*

Little children, come and play
for a little while.

English

A stranger came and scattered
the playing stones.

Contextual Considerations

- I learned this song from Kenyan ethnomusicologist Dr. Jean Kidula.
- This call-and-response song was originally sung in Swahili (also seen as KiSwahili, meaning the language of Swahili) and was then appropriated in Luo and Luhya, two of the dialects spoken in Kenya.
- Dr. Kidula explained that the song is present in other singing cultures in Kenya with verses added (such as seen here with the verse in Luhya).
- *Marobo* means stones, and the song can be used as a rock-passing game. Choose a pattern that works for you and your students.

Music in **Tanzania**

Tanzania has many ethnic groups, including the *Wangoni* (Wa at the beginning of the word means people— so *Wangoni* means "the Ngoni people"), *Wamakonde*, and *Wahehe* from the south; the *Wasukuma* near Lake Victoria, the *Wanyamwezi* from the west; the *Wagogo* from central Tanzania; the *Wasambaa* from the northeast; and the *Wazanzibari* from the islands of Zanzibar off the coast. There are more than 120 ethnic groups, each

with their own distinct music traditions. There are songs for many occasions, including work, harvest, hunting, puberty, lullabies, battle, religion, weddings, funerals, therapy, love, games, and baby naming.

The most common time signature throughout the country is 6/8, although 2/4 is found here and there. A common scale is a pentatonic variant (such as *do re mi sol la do'*). A notable exception is in Wagogo music, which features the descending tritone in most traditional songs. Other genres include *muziki wa dansi* (dance music) and *bongo flava* (considered to be youth music and showing heavy influence from U.S. and European pop genres). *Kwaya* (gospel choir) is a staple on the radio, and from Zanzibar comes *taarab* with its obvious Arabic influences.

The song and chant included here were taught to me by Dr. Kedmon Mapana of the University of Dar es Salaam in Tanzania. In addition to his professorial duties, he is the founder and director of the Chamwino Arts Center, which is dedicated to celebrating traditional Wagogo music and dance throughout the year and in a special multi-day festival each July.

Maludeje

Fragment Singing – Call and Response
Movement with the Beat

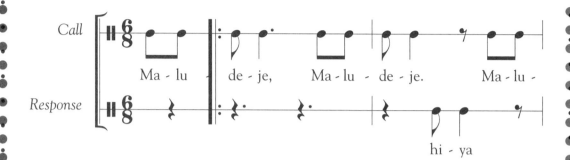

Call

Ma - lu - de - je, Ma - lu - de - je. Ma - lu -

Response

hi - ya

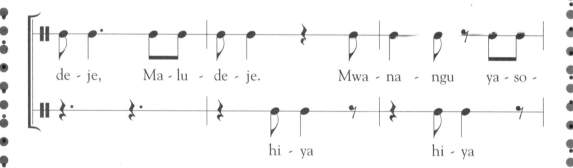

de - je, Ma - lu - de - je. Mwa - na - ngu ya - so -

hi - ya hi - ya

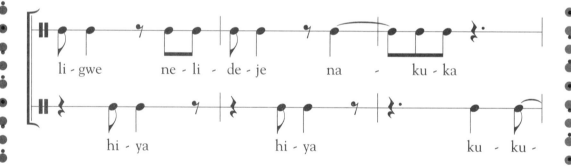

li - gwe ne - li - de - je na - ku - ka

hi - ya hi - ya ku - ku -

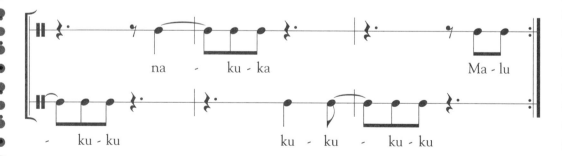

na - ku - ka Ma - lu

- ku - ku ku - ku - ku - ku

Cigogo	English
Maludeje, Maludeje. (2x) *Mah-loo-deh-jeh*	A kite!
Hiya! *Hee-yah*	Oh no!
Mwanangu *Mwah-nahn-goo*	My child
yasoligwe *yah-soh-leeg-weh*	has been taken
nelideje *Neh-lee-deh-jeh*	by the kite!
nakuka* *Nah-koo-kah*	I tried to protect it!
kuku *Koo-koo*	*action of protection

Movement Instructions

1. All kneel on the ground with hands on the floor in front, pecking toward the ground like chickens on the beat.
2. When the chickens answer "Hiya!," children sit up quickly with hands up in the air and then return quickly to pecking around.
3. When the chickens answer "Kuku," children arch their backs up and down on the beat, with the head moving in sync.

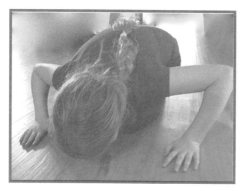

Pecking at the ground

Hiya!

Kuku

Kuku

Mbukwenyi

Fragment Singing – Call and Response
Movement with the Beat

Call

Mbu - kwe - nyi wa - do - do mbu - kwe - nyi wa - do - do

Response   *Call*

Mbu - kwa, mbu - kwa   Mbu - kwa, mbu - kwa   Wa -

Response

nyi - na ze - nyu   wa - bi - ta ha - i   Wa -

bi - te tu - mba   wa - bi - te tu - mba

Call

(i)tu - mba ku - ko   k(u)so - la chi - chi

Response

k(u)so - la sa - nga   k(u)so - la sa - nga

Call

Sa - nga zi - zo za - chi ze - ne

Response

Za ku - vi - ni - la m - do - mo - do - mo.

Call

Mdo - mo wu - wo wa - vi - na - ga nha - u - le

Response

nha - vi nha - vi - vi nha - vi nha - vi - vi

nha - vi nha - vi - vi nha - vi nha - vi - vi

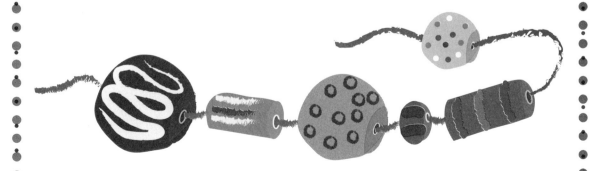

Cigogo	English
(Call) Mbukwenyi, wadodo (2x) *(M)boo-kwehn-yee wah-doh-doh*	Good morning, children.
(Response) Mbukwa, mbukwa (5x) *(M)boo-kwa(m) boo-kwa*	Good morning!
Call: Wanyina zenyu wabita hai? *Wah-nyee-nah zeh-nyoo wah-bee-tah hah-ee*	Where has your mother gone?
Response: Wabite tumba (2x) *Wah-bee-teh toom-bah*	To the anthill place.
Call: (i)tumba kuko k(u)sola chichi? *Ee-toom-bah koo-koh koo-soh-lah chee-chee*	What is happening there?
Response: K(u)sola sanga (2x) *Koo-soh-lah sahn-gah*	She went to buy beads.
Call: Sanga zizo zachi zene? *Sahn-gah zee-zoh zah-chee zeh-neh*	Why is she buying beads?
Response: Za kuvinila mdomodomo. *Zah koo-vee-nee-lah(m) doh-mo-doh-mo*	For the neck dance.
Call: Mdomo wuwo wavinaga nhaule? *(m)doh-moh woo-woh wah-vee-nah-gah n(h)a-oo-leh*	How do you do the neck dance?
Response: Nhavi nhavivi (4x) *N(h)a-vee n(h)a-vee-vee*	Like this!

Contextual Considerations

- This song tells the story of the women going off to buy beads to make long necklaces used in a particular dance known as *mdomodomo*. The market is located near the place where there are tall anthills. When the children are asked how they dance, they emulate the motion the women make during mdomodomo. The women wear a long, thin strand of white beads. By leaning over and moving their heads back and forth, they are able to get the necklace spinning in circles around their necks, much like a hula-hoop around the hips.
- Mdomodomo is accompanied with singing, instruments, and dancing, and is performed by males and females.

Teaching Considerations

- This song has more words than most in the collection. The first two response lines are the easiest for a start.
- Consider ways to minimize the work for the children by leading the call yourself, or perhaps splitting the children into groups, with each learning a line or two.
- Use the song in a number of classes so the words become more and more familiar over time.

Movement Instructions

- During the song, swing arms back and forth on the beat.
- On "nhavi," clap hands on beat 1. Note that this phrase switches into 3/4.
- On "nhavivi," put hand to forehead as in a salute and push chin and face forward on beats 2 and 3.

Swing arms

Nhavi

Nhavivi

South Africa

South Africa includes the following countries:

Angola

Botswana

Eswatini
  (formerly Swaziland)

Lesotho

Malawi

Mozambique

Namibia

South Africa

Zambia

Zimbabwe

The larger ethnic groups throughout the area include the Xhosa, Zulu, Tsonga, Swazi, Ndebele, Sotho, and Shona. There was much colonization throughout South Africa leading to the additional presence of a large European population.

Music in Zimbabwe

Marimba music is popular in Zimbabwe even though it has only existed since the 1960s. A group of educators at a music academy were concerned that older music traditions would be lost as people moved from the rural villages into the larger cities. There was also concern about the segregated colonial education system that did not teach local traditional music in school. To address these concerns, an academy for the study of traditional music was founded and was called *Kwanongoma* (the place where drums are played or the place of singing). While the marimba was more prevalent in neighboring Zambia and Mozambique, it was selected to be a teaching instrument at *Kwanongoma*. It was deemed to be distinctly African in that it had not been commandeered by the colonial government. In addition to marimbas, *mbira* (thumb pianos)—a traditional instrument of the Shona people—were given a prominent role in the curriculum.

Music played an important role through protest songs during the fight for independence. Thomas Mapfumo is one of the leading songwriters with more than 40 years of activism through songs in a genre known as *Chimurenga*. Folk traditions and contemporary styles are found side by side, and they are combined together.

Yave Nguva Yezhizha

Fragment Singing

Movement with the Beat

Ya - ve ngu - va ye - zhi - zha   Ya - ve ngu - va ye - zhi - zha

Ya - ve ngu - va ye - zhi - zha   Ti - koh - we.   Ti - koh - we   Ndi -

ri - ni?   Ndi - ra Ku - ka - dzi Ku - ru   me Kub -

vum - bi.   Ndi - ra Ku - ka - dzi Ku - ru - me Kub - vum - bi.*   Ndi

* indicates the final note after any number of repeats

Shona	English
Yave nguva yezhizha (3x) *Yah-vehn goo-vah yeh-zhee-zha*	It is rainy season
Tikohwe *Tee-koh-weh*	Reap.
Ndirini? *(n)dih-ree-nee*	When is it?
Ndira *(n)dee-rah*	January
Kukadzi *Koo-kah-dzee*	February
Kurume *Koo-roo-meh*	March
Kubvumbi *Kuhb-voom-bee*	April

Teaching Considerations
- The (n) means to start the word with a closed "n" sound—not "ehn."
- The whole group sings "Yave nguva yezhizha."
- One child calls "Ndirini?"
- Perform solos for each month, or duets, or small groups.
- Add a movement for each month, eventually taking away the words and just presenting the movements one at a time in place of the lyrics.

Selected Resources for Music from Africa

Recordings

Ghana:
African Songs & Rhythms for Children. (1990).
    Smithsonian Folkways Records. https://s.si.edu/31sZrTy
Ewe Music of Ghana. (1969/2004).
    Smithsonian Folkways Records. https://s.si.edu/31rPZ2K
Folk Music of Ghana. (1964).
    Smithsonian Folkways Records. https://s.si.edu/2Krilo8
Ghana Children at Play. (1976/2004).
    Smithsonian Folkways Records. https://s.si.edu/2ZQpUtO
Music of the Ashanti of Ghana. (1979/2004).
    Smithsonian Folkways Records. https://s.si.edu/2MhdRCT

Kenya:
Children's Songs from Kenya. (1975).
    Folkways Records. https://s.si.edu/2OPx0xM
Gospel Songs from Kenya. (1976).
    Folkways Records. https://s.si.edu/2OKw2Tg
Music of the Waswahili of Lamu, Kenya (3 Volumes). (1985).
    Folkways Records. https://s.si.edu/2MXk0TU

Tanzania:
Sing to the Well: Wagogo People Tanzania. (2005).
    Voices from the Nations.
Tanzania: Chants Wagogo. (2011).
    Collection Ocora.

Books/Articles

African Songs and Rhythms for Children.
    By W. K. Omoaku. Schott Publications.
Kenya Sing and Dance.
    By Tim Gregory. http://timgregory.org/about.html

Let Your Voice Be Heard. (1997).
    By Abraham Adzeniyah, Dumisani Maraire, and Judith Cook Tucker.
    Danbury, CT: World Music Press.
Music in West Africa: Experiencing Music, Expressing Culture. (2005).
    By Ruth M. Stone. New York: Oxford Music Press.
Musical Labor Performed in Northwest Tanzania. (2015).
    By Frank Gunderson. https://s.si.edu/2ORyJT2
Sowah Mensah. Materials available through www.sowahmensah.com
    Adenkum. (2009). A group of songs and chants.
    Welcome Song. (2009). A piece for gyil (Ghanaian xylophones).
    Sii Sii Sii. (2010). Arrangement for singing and drums.
    Sowah's Drum Sequence. (2016). Learn the basic fundamentals of Ghanaian
        music.
    Salabi Ye. (2017). Children's song with accompanying DVD.

Videos

iASO Records. (January 12, 2007).
    Kora music from West African Griot lankandia cissoko. [YouTube video].
    https://bit.ly/2MfOX6k
Musical Labor Performed in Northwest Tanzania. (2015).
    https://s.si.edu/2yNRrjR
Por Por Honk Horn Music of Ghana: The La Drivers Union Por Por Group. (2007).
    https://s.si.edu/2ON8uxd
SublimeWorldProd. (August 28, 2014). Sounds from Ghana. [YouTube video].
    https://bit.ly/2yRyLzD
theghanaproject2013. (March 10, 2014). Sample video of Ghanaian traditional
    music. [YouTube video]. https://bit.ly/2KB7w1O
This World Music.
    https://bit.ly/31pKqSg_

*Convenient links to online resources listed here are also available at GIA Publications
website. Visit www.giamusic.com/firststepsglobal.*

MUSIC FROM
Oceania

Philippine Sea

Northern Mariana islands (U.S.)

Guam (U.S.)

PALAU

FEDERATED STATES OF MICRONESIA

MARSHALL ISLANDS

NAURU

KIRIBATI

S I A

PAPUA NEW GUINEA

★ Port Moresby

SOLOMON ISLANDS

Honiara

TUVALU

Tokelau (N.Z.)

SAMOA

MOR-STE

Coral Sea

VANUATU

FIJI

Suva ★

FRENCH POLYNESIA

TONGA

New Caledonia (FRANCE)

Noumea ★

Alice Springs

U S T R A L I A

AUSTRALIA

Kermadec islands (N.Z.)

Sydney

Lord Howe Island (AUSTL.)

Canberra ★

Great Australian Bight

Melbourne

Tasman Sea

NEW ZEALAND

NEW ZEALAND

Wellington ★

Tasmania

Chatham islands (N.Z.)

Oceania

Oceania is comprised of Australasia, Melanesia, Micronesia, and Polynesia covering over 3 million miles. Even though Oceania covers such a vast distance, it contains the smallest land area and the second smallest population after Antarctica. Different clusters of islands have been colonized by different countries over the centuries, so there are common characteristics due to indigenous cultures and geography, and then variations based on the influence of the individual colonizing cultures.

The countries in Oceania include:

Australia	Micronesia	Papua New Guinea	Tuvalu
Fiji	Nauru	Samoa	Vanuatu
Kiribati	New Zealand	Solomon Islands	Zimbabwe
Marshall Islands	Palau	Tonga	

The different countries are made of many islands. For example, the Federated States of Micronesia has more than 600 islands.

Music in **Tahiti**

Tahiti is the largest island in French Polynesia, an overseas collectivity of France that consists of more than 100 islands. French Polynesia is divided into different archipelagos (island groupings), including the Austral, Gambier, Marquesas, Society, and Tuamotu Islands spread across more than 1,600 miles. Tahiti has the largest population with close to 70 percent of the population of French Polynesia.

TAHITIAN PERCUSSION ENSEMBLE INSTRUMENTS: FA'ATETE, TO'ERE, PAHU

A popular song form in Tahiti is *'aparima* with its beautiful hand gestures that tell the story of the lyrics. Also well loved is the percussion ensemble, including large slit logs (*to'ere*), a medium drum that plays fast-moving rhythms (*fa'atete*), and a bass-type drum (*pahu*). This ensemble often accompanies the *dance ote'a* with the women's fast hip movements and the men's knee movements. *Himene* are choirs that sing multipart hymns (upward of 8 parts!) with a distinctly Tahitian sound. Ukuleles and guitars are commonly featured in song accompaniments. A great opportunity to see the wide range of music traditions is the annual festival known as *Heiva* held in the month of July. Music and dance ensembles from across French Polynesia come to compete in a beautiful outdoor arena.

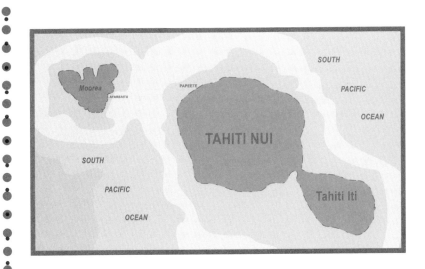

Poreho
Songtales

Po - re - ho _____ no ro-to o'-e - i te mi - ti _____

Ma a' o - e na te ____ fe 'e ____ A - mu-hi - a o' - e

te fe - 'e ____ A - na pa - na-pa mai To 'o -

e, a - pu-i - ti e. A - na pa - na-pa mai, To 'o -

e A-pu-i-ti e Po - re -

Teaching Considerations

- Gather images of octopus and crabs to create a slide show.
- I often put the words on the slides in a large font regardless of the age of the students to support word recognition and reading development (and to help myself with songs in less familiar languages).
- Some children will already be reading, some will still be learning basic letter recognition, and some will not yet be ready for connecting sight to sound.

Tahitian

Poreho no roto o'ei te miti
Poh-reh-ho no ro-to o-eh ee teh mee-tee

Ma a' oe na te fe'e
Mah-ah o-eh nah-teh feh-eh

Amuhia o'e te fe'e
Ah-moo hee-ah o-eh teh feh-eh

Ana panapa mai!
Ah-nah pah nah pah mah-ee

To 'oe apuiti e
Toh o-eh ah-poo ee-ee eh

English

Shellfish, you live in the sea.

You are the octopus' dinner.

You are eaten by the octopus.

Your radiance!

Your shell! *

* similar to a tiger shell

Taoto

Simple Songs

Tao - to, pe - pe, Tao - to te pe - pe

tao - to e. E - ra ma - ma tai te a' au.

E - ra pa - pa tai te pe - ho, E ti' - i a - tu ra

i te fe' i, Ha - ma - ni po - po - i na' a - iu.

Tahitian	English
Taoto, pepe, *Toh-toh, peh-peh*	Sleep, baby,
Taoto te pepe taoto e. *Toh-toh tay peh-peh toh-toh eh*	Sleep baby sleep, yes.
Era mama tai te a' au. *Eh-rah mama tayee tay ah ah-oo*	Mama went to the reef.
Era papa tai te peho, *Eh-rah papa tayee teh peh-ho*	Papa went to the valley,
E ti'i atu ra i te fe' i, *Eh tee-ee ah-too-rah ee-teh feh-ee*	to pick plantains,
Hamani popoi na' aiu. *Ha-mah-nee poh-poh-ee nah ah-yoo*	to make baby's porridge.

Teaching Considerations

- Have children listen for particular words as you are singing (e.g., mama, pepe). This engages them in actively listening during multiple repeats.
- Have children sing only particular words. You can use a visual for this and underline the special words, adding, subtracting, and increasing the challenge over multiple classes as they take over more and more.
- It does not matter whether or not children are able to read fluently. Using a visual helps to support those who are identifying letters and sounds, and gives you a visual cue to point at or signal.
- Have children create motions to reflect the story.

Music in **New Zealand**

When discussing traditional songs from New Zealand, Maori practices are the most well known. Traditional Maori songs are organized by use and group songs are often sung in unison. These include chanted spells (*karakia*), pre-speechmaking songs (*tauparapara*), a guard's song (*wahakaaraara paa*), women's response to rumors (*paatere*), and a song to express distaste for enemies (*kaioraora*).

The most well-known musical form from New Zealand is the *haka*, a dance of postures with shouted accompaniment. It has become a symbol of New Zealand, most often associated with football and public celebrations. The haka was not just a war dance, nor was it only performed by men. There are even simple haka for children.

Po Atarau

Movement with the Beat

Movement for Form and Expression

Teaching Considerations

- The internal form of this piece (a, b, a, c, or b¹) lends itself to movement ideas that express each element. Consider perhaps a different simple movement for each letter, or split the children into groups: one for a, one for b, etc.
- The children can create a movement for their phrase/section.
- The different ending on the last phrase offers the opportunity to discuss the similarity with the second phrase.

Maori	English
Po atarau *Poh ah-tah-rah-oo*	Now is the hour
e moea iho nei *Eh moh-eh-ah ee-ho neh-ee*	for me to say goodbye
E haere ana *Eh hah-eh-reh ah-nah*	Soon you'll be sailing
Koe ki pamamao *Koh-eh kee pah-mah-mah-oh*	Far across the sea.
Haere ra *Ha-eh-reh rah*	While you're away
Kahoki mai ano *Kah ho-kee mah-ee ah-noh*	Kindly remember me
Ki te tau *Kee teh tah-oo*	When you return
E tangi atu nei *Eh tahn-gee ah-too neh-ee*	You will find me waiting here

Music in **Australia**

From Australia, it seems fitting to start with music of the indigenous peoples, from which we have the unique and celebrated *didgeridoo* (wooden wind instrument). Throughout Aboriginal communities, there are songs for hunting, funerals, gossiping, animals, seasons, ancestral stories, myths, and Dreamtime stories.

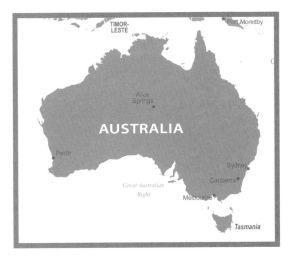

Dreamtime refers to the Aboriginal belief that all life (human, animal, bird, and fish) is part of one large network that can be traced back to the spirit ancestors. This continues as the dreaming in spiritual practice for Aboriginal people in contemporary society. Ancient events and ancestors are depicted and connected to the present through dance and chanted song verses, and they may be accompanied by the didgeridoo.

After colonization and Westernization, British influence started to create hybrids with local traditions. Sea shanties found their way into the song canon along with other ballads and social songs. Rock, pop, and country music are popular throughout the country, and fusion groups are respected for their contributions honoring traditional and new musical practices.

Click Go the Shears

Songtales

Out on the boards, me lads, a blade shear - er stands,

Grasp - ing his shears in his thin bo - ny hands, and his

blear - y eyes are fixed on a blue bel - lied yoe,

"If I on - ly get you I will make the rin - ger go!"

Click go the shears, boys, click click click!

Wide is the blow and his hands move__ quick, And the

rin - ger looks a-round, and he's bea-ten by a blow, And he

cur - ses the old snag-ger with the blue__ bel - lied yoe!

Out on the boards, me lads, a blade shearer stands,
Grasping his shears in his thin bony hands,
And his bleary eyes are fixed on a blue bellied yoe,
"If I only get you I will make the ringer go!"

Chorus:

Click go the shears, boys, click, click, click!
Wide is the blow and his hands move quick,
And the ringer looks around, and he's beaten by a blow,
And he curses the old snagger* with the blue bellied yoe!*

Out on the floor in a cane-bottomed chair
Sits the boss of the board with his eyes everywhere,
He looks at each fleece as it comes to the screen,
Saying, "For goodness' sake, can't you take them off clean?"

The tar-boy is there, waiting on demand,
With his tarry jam pot and his stick in his hand;
He sees an old merino with a cut upon her back,
This is what he's waiting for, "Oh, tar here, Jack!"

You take off the belly wool, finickle* out the crutch,*
Then go up the neck, for the rules they are such;
Clean around the horns, and the first shoulder down,
A long blow up the back and then turn around.

* "Snagger" is a local word for "shearer."
* "Yoe" is a dialect word for "ewe."
* "Finickle" means to finish.
* "Crutch" is the hind legs; "crutching" would be removing the
   wool from the hind legs.

OCEANIA

Contextual Considerations

- Sheep shearing is a frequent topic in folk songs from Australia, ranging from tales of the shearers (both good and bad), to record-winning numbers of sheep shorn, to tales of dogs jumping in the piles of fleece to chew on it.
- This songtale tells the story of a competition between shearers. The reigning champion finds himself beaten by an older, less successful shearer who was fortunate to pick a sheep with less wool than the others.
- While this song is in English, it is loaded with vocabulary that may be unfamiliar.
  - Create slides with pictures to help move the song along and introduce the words. I have found success in giving the clicker to a student so I can continue to accompany on an instrument.
  - As with all songtales, students can also draw original artwork to create a class songbook, or they can create individual songbooks to take home.
  - Additionally, you can scan a class songbook and send it to the parents as a digital file for at-home music-making.

Selected Resources for Music from Oceania

Websites

https://www.aboriginalart.com.au/didgeridoo/
    Introduction to traditional Aboriginal music.
https://www.heiva.org/en/home/
    This is the website for Heiva, the Tahitian music festival.

Recordings

Australia: Aboriginal Music. (1977).
    Smithsonian Folkways Records. https://s.si.edu/2Ks1ulg
Australian Ballads: The Early Years. (1981).
    Smithsonian Folkways Records. https://s.si.edu/2TiQ9qi
Australia: Music from the New England Tablelands of New South Wales, 1850-1900. (1998).
    Smithsonian Folkways Records. https://s.si.edu/2yNeV8A
Maori Songs of New Zealand. (1952).
    Smithsonian Folkways Recordings. https://s.si.edu/2GWZW0o
Royal Tahitian Dance Company. (1974).
    Smithsonian Folkways Recordings. https://s.si.edu/2YTCX0s
Songs of Aboriginal Australia and Torres Straits. (1964).
    Smithsonian Folkways Records. https://s.si.edu/2Mde4qj

Books/Articles

10 Classic New Zealand Children's Books.
    https://bit.ly/2YURqJk
100 Best Kiwi Children's Books.
    https://bit.ly/31FxTdO
Diversity in Australia's Music: Themes Past, Present, and for the Future. (2018).
    By Doryotta Fabian and John Napier (Eds.). Cambridge Scholars Publishing.
Houkulele Tahitian & Polynesian Songbook.
    https://bit.ly/2KxzooD
Maori Music. (1996). By Mervyn McLean. Auckland University Press.

Videos

AIG. (October 6, 2014). *Haka-History*
[YouTube Video]. https://bit.ly/2H7WnEN
Spirit Gallery. (September 28, 2013). *Didgeridoo Meets Orchestra*
[YouTube Video]. https://bit.ly/2TyR7im
Tahiti Nui Télévision. (July 20, 2018). *Heiva i Tahiti 2018 – Soirée des lauréats*
[YouTube Video]. https://bit.ly/2MhGXBV

Convenient links to online resources listed here are also available at GIA Publications website. Visit www.giamusic.com/firststepsglobal.

MUSIC FROM
Asia

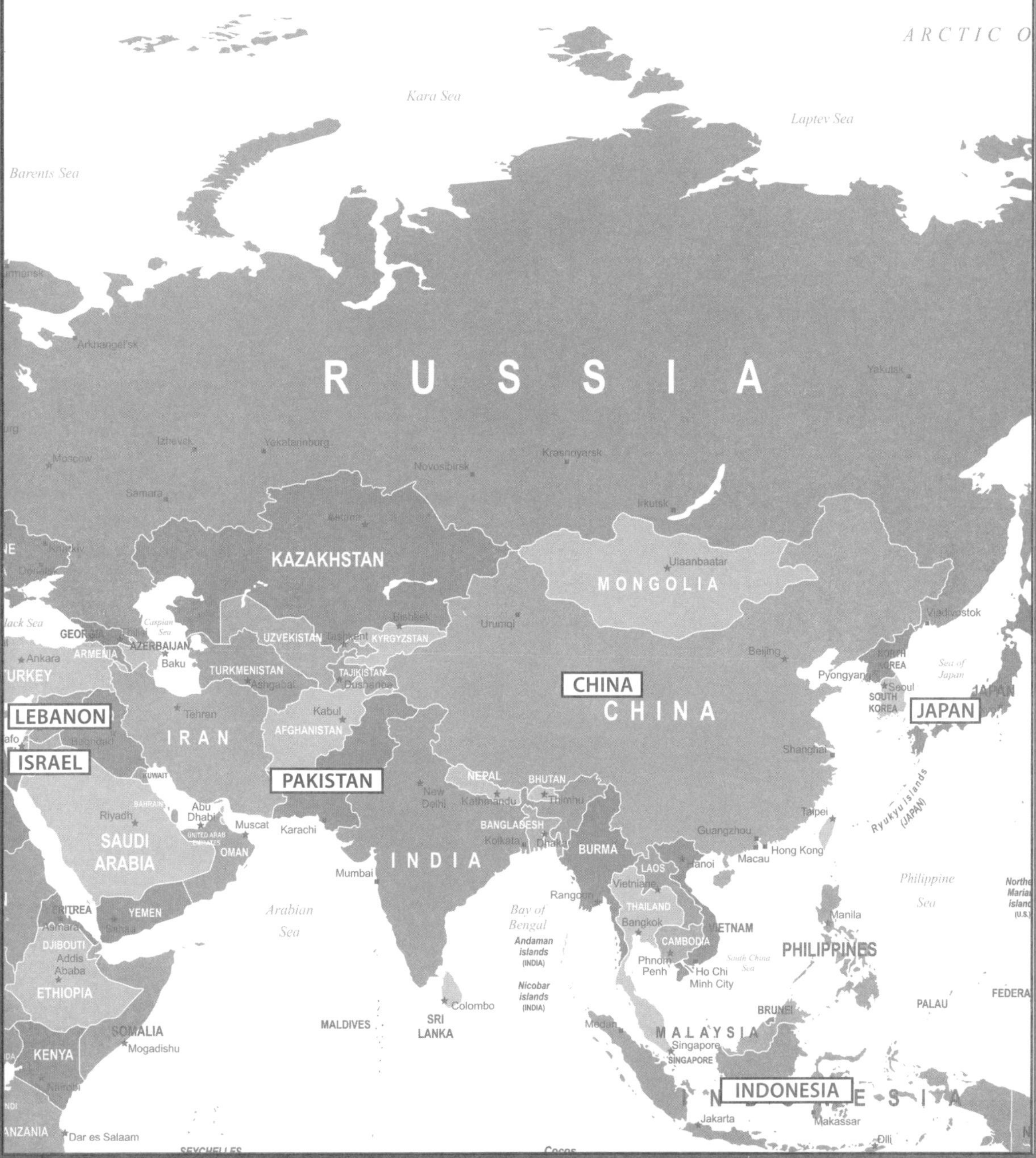

Asia

Asia is the largest and most populous continent covering about 30 percent of total land area. There are 50 countries, with some considered to be both Asian and European:

Azerbaijan   Georgia   Kazakhstan   Russia
Turkey

Russia occupies about 30 percent of the continent. Two other counties are technically in Asia yet considered to be a part of Europe:

Armenia   Cyprus

The remaining countries include (alphabetically):

Afghanistan	Israel	Nepal	Syria
Bahrain	Japan	North Korea	Taiwan
Bangladesh	Jordan	Oman	Tajikistan
Bhutan	Kuwait	Pakistan	Thailand
Brunei	Kyrgyzstan	Palestine	Timor-Leste
Cambodia	Laos	Philippines	Turkmenistan
China	Lebanon	Qatar	United Arab Emirates
India	Malaysia	Saudi Arabia	Uzbekistan
Indonesia	Maldives	Singapore	Vietnam
Iran	Mongolia	South Korea	Yemen
Iraq	Myanmar	Sri Lanka	

Just reading through this list of countries brings to mind a broad spectrum of languages, religions and, certainly, musical soundscapes.

Music in **China**

There is a long history of both classical and folk music in China. Classical music is typically associated with poetry or philosophy and is played on instruments such as the *guqin* (plucked zither) or the *pipa* (lute). These practices are taught orally between master teacher and student. There are notated versions of music, but students usually learn aurally first. It is only in the last century that classical music left elite society and became music for all people.

Folk songs are divided into several categories, but there is often overlap between:

Haozi (work songs)   *Wu'ge* (dance songs)
Shan'ge (mountain songs)   *Yu'ge* (Fisherman's songs)
Xiaodiao (small or rural tunes)

Not to be left out are ritual songs, vendors' cries, long songs, religious songs, story songs, and children's songs.

There are many ethnic groups throughout China, each with unique folk traditions. Classical music is typically instrumental, but folk music also includes vocals for love songs and stories. Silk and Bamboo ensembles are heard regularly as well as regional opera. Many contemporary songs have drawn inspiration from the vast repertoire of folk music.

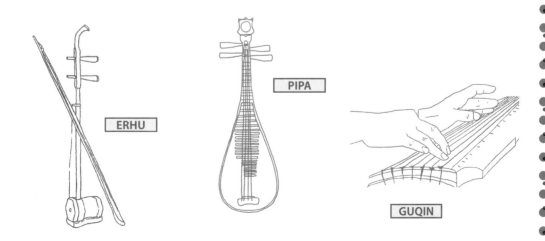

Mo Li Hua

Movement with the Beat

Songtale

Hau yi duo mei li de mo li hua

fen fang mei li man jy ya,

Yeou shiang yeou bai ren ren kua

Rang wo lai jiang ni jai shia

sung gei bie ren jia, mo li

hua mo li hua

Mandarin (*transliterated*)	**English**
Hau yi duo mei li de mo li hua *Hah-oo yee doh meh-ee lee dee moh lee hwa*	Such a beautiful jasmine flower.
Fen fang mei li man jy ya. *Fehn fahng meh lee man joo* yah*	Branches full of sweet white buds.
Yeou shiang yeou bai ren ren kua, *Yoh shyahng yoh bah-ee zhen zhen kwa*	Everyone loves their beauty,
Rang wo lai jiang ni jai shia *Rahng woh lah-ee tyahng nee tsah-ee shee-ah*	I will gather some and offer them
Sung gei bie ren jia, *Sohng geh-ee byeh ren chyah*	to the one I love,
Mo li hua, Mo li hua. *Moh lee hwa, Moh lee hwa.*	Jasmine Flower, Jasmine Flower.

Teaching Considerations

- The first "h" in "*Hah*" is breathy.
- Sing "oo" as in "book."
- Have the children listen as you sing and count the number of times they hear "mo li hua," which means jasmine flower. Perhaps have a picture of a jasmine flower visible. This may likely take more than one time through the song for careful listening (4 times).
- Ask the children to listen again and compare the 4 times they hear "mo li hua." Are they the same? Are they different? (The first two are the same; the last two are different).
- When the children correctly figure out that the last two are different, ask them to describe the difference.
- Have children sing the first two "mo li huas," and you sing the rest.
- When done successfully, add the third "mo li hua" for the children. When accurate, add the fourth.
- These repeated repetitions allow the rest of the lyrics to be heard again and again while the children are actively focused on a task. When you are ready, begin to add more lyrics. This does not need to happen in one or two classes, but can happen slowly over several meetings.

Music in **Japan**

Japan features pop, rock, gospel music, and other contemporary traditions. There are also thriving classical and traditional music traditions with long histories. The *koto* (zither), *shakuhachi* (bamboo flute), and *shamizen* (plucked and strummed string instrument) are the most recognizable instruments and can be studied in music conservatories or in the master/apprentice model of teaching and learning.

Several theatrical forms feature live music, including *Noh* and *Kabuki* (opera forms) and *Bunraku* (puppet theater). A respected classical music is an ancient court genre called *Gaguku* featuring flutes, plucked string instruments, and drums and gongs.

Matsuri (festivals) are featured throughout the country with live music, including singing, instruments, and dancing with community members joining in the fun. Some of the larger festivals include:

- *Gion Matsuri* for the whole month of July
- *Awa Odori* – the largest traditional dance festival in Japan
- *Nebuta Matsuri* – includes thousands of chanting dancers
- *Kochi Yosakoi* – based on the dance created to accompany the old song *Yosakoi Bushi*
- *Tanabata* – based on the Chinese legend about two stars

Taiko, an ancient percussion genre, has gained popularity around the world with drums ranging from the small, higher-pitched *shime* to the largest, the *odaiko*.

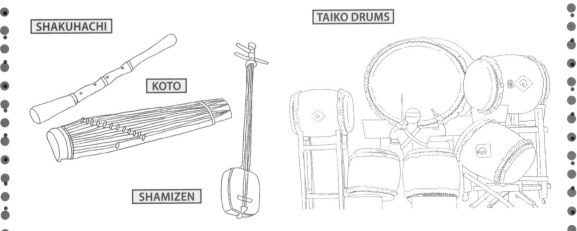

Cradle Song

Movement for Form and Expression

Yu   ri   ka   go   no   u   ta   o

ka   na   ri   ya   ga   u   ta   u   yo

Ne   n   ne   ko - ne   n   ne   ko

Ne   n   ne   ko   yo

first steps in global music

Japanese	English
Yu ri ka go no u ta o	A canary sings a cradle lullaby.
Yoo ree kah goh no hoo tah oh	
Ka na ri ya ga u ta u yo	
Kah nah ree yah gah oo tah oo yoh	
Ne n ne kone n ne ko	Sleep, baby, sleep.
Neh n neh koh-neh n neh –koh	
Ne n ne ko yo	Sleep, baby, sleep.
Neh n neh koh yoh	

Teaching Considerations

- A solo "n" is pronounced closed, not "ehn."
- This tune lends itself to aural analysis and comparison, as none of the phrases are the same.
- Challenge the children to sing different notes (the first pitch of each phrase, the last phrase).
- Play an "in and out" type of game where you sing certain sounds and then signal for when the children should sing.

Kirisu

Simple Songs

Ki - ri - su, chon!　　Ki - ri - su, chon!

Ko - do - mo - ni　to - ra - re - te　a - ho - ra - shi, chon!

Japanese	**English**
Kirisu, chon! (2x)	Grasshopper, hop!
Kee-ree-soo, chohn!	
Kodomoni torarete	Keep hopping until you get to me!
Koh-doh-moh-nee toh-rah-reh-the	
Ahorashi, chon!	
Ah-hoh-rah-shee, chohn!	

Game Instructions

- Children walk in a circle.
- One child is the *kirisu* (grasshopper) and hops in the opposite direction inside the circle.
- On the last note of the song, the kirisu taps a child in the circle who then follows along.
- On the last note, the second child taps a third to join, and so on.

Music in **Pakistan**

Music in Pakistan is diverse, as is the population with a history going back over 5,000 years. With genres ranging from rock to *qawwali* (a devotional music based in Sufi Islam), and genres showing influence from neighboring countries in Central Asia, one can hear a wide range of influences, combinations, old traditions, and new creations.

There are many instruments in Pakistan, including stringed instruments such as the *sarod, sitar, rebab*; wind instruments such as the *pungi*, and *been*; and percussion instruments such as *tabla, dholak, dhol*, and *khunjari*. Classical songs are often quite emotional with love as a frequent topic. Folk songs in Pakistan deal with topics related to daily life.

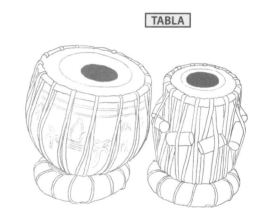

TABLA

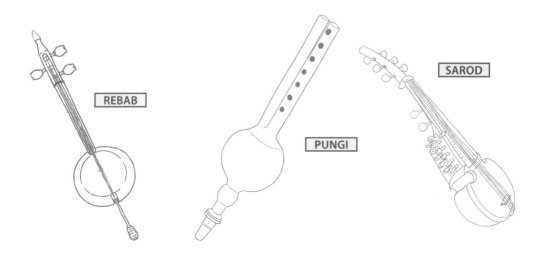

REBAB

PUNGI

SAROD

Ache Kuwwa

Movement with the Beat

Urdu	English
Ache kuwwa piyasa tha *eighk kuh-wuh pee-yah-sah tuh*	There was a thirsty crow.
Jug meh Pani thoda tha *juhg meh pah-nee toh-duh tuh*	The pail had very little water.
Kuwwa neh dala kunkar *kuh-wuh neigh tah-lah kuhn-kur*	The crow put pebbles in.
Pani aya uper *pah-nee ai-yuh oo-per*	The water rose up!
Kuwwa neh piya Pani *kuw-wuh neigh pee-yuh pah-nee*	The crow drank the water.
Khatam hui our Kahani *(h)uh-tuhm hoo-ee ar kah-hah-nee*	That's the end of our story.

Contextual Considerations

- This tune is sung in Urdu, which is the national language of Pakistan, and it is one of the many languages spoken throughout the country.
- The lyrics are based on the fable *The Crow and The Pitcher*, which extols the virtue of ingenuity. There are many children's books based on the story. As with any of these songs, new versions of the books can be assembled with original student artwork and the new language inserted.
- Another option is to read the book in English and then use the song to create an extended form.

Teaching Considerations

- The "t" in Urdu does not aspirate the way a "t" does in English. Listen to the recording to help you hear the difference.

Music in **Indonesia**

Indonesia has one of the largest populations in the world with more than 300 ethnic groups, almost as many languages, and some 3,000 populated islands out of more than 13,000 in the archipelago. About 90 percent of Indonesians are Muslim, and there are

Christians, Buddhists, and Hindus. Certainly, this leads to a music culture as diverse as the population. The most recognized are the percussion orchestras from Java and Bali, called *gamelan*, consisting of gongs, metallophones, drum, and combined with singing and elegant, intricate dance. Singing involves solos and group arrangements, and one can also hear flutes and zithers. Brass bands are found alongside guitars, Christian hymns, and court music. There are scales and forms in gamelan that are uniquely Indonesian, and then other forms that show influence from outside cultures and influences.

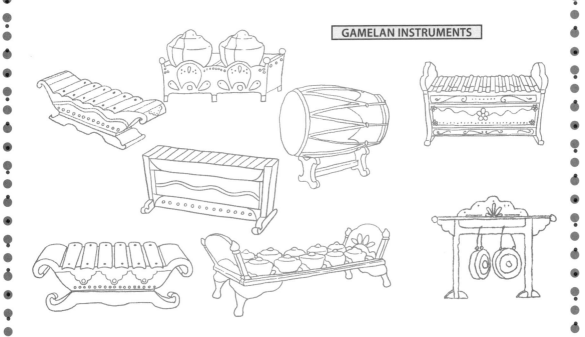

GAMELAN INSTRUMENTS

O Anane Kéké

Movement with the Beat

O - yi - na - ni ké - ké, mo - ké mo -

sa - kú No - ri - va ké - ké i -

ma___ tu - mo ru - gma la - lo

Ué - a - né, Ué - a - né, Ué - a -

né ké - ké Oa - ni - ma si -

a pa - pa___ sa - ne - mo o - si - é

Contextual Considerations

- According to Javanese gamelan specialist Joko Sutrisno, *O Anane Kéké* is from the Minahasa ethnic group in North Sulawesi, Indonesia, not far from the southernmost point of the Philippines.

Minahasan

Oyinani kéké, moké mosakú,
Oh-ee-nah-nee keh-keh, moh-keh moh-sah-koo

Noriva kéké ima tumo rugma lalo,
Noh-ree-vah keh-keh ee-mah too-moh roo-gmah lay-loh

Uéané, uéané, uéané kéké,
way-ah-neh, way-ah-neh, way-ah-neh keh-keh

Oanima sia papa sanemo osié.
Oh-nee-mah see-ah pah-pah sah-neh-moh oh-see-eh

English (general)

Go to sleep. All my love is for you

and I protect you in my arms.

Middle East

The Middle East is unique as a region in that it reaches into three continents: Asia, Europe, and Africa. Countries in the Middle East include:

Bahrain	Oman
Cyprus	Palestine
Egypt	Qatar
Iran	Saudi Arabia
Iraq	Syria
Israel	Turkey
Jordan	United Arab Emirates
Kuwait	Yemen
Lebanon	

Music in Israel

Classical orchestras, choirs, and opera are important in the cultural life of Israel. Immigration in Israel has happened in waves since the 1880s, each bringing cultures to meet with other cultures, including the existing community in Palestine before the establishment of the State of Israel. Traditional folk music shows influence from all of the cultures that have contributed over the decades. Songs are often in Hebrew or Arabic, and other languages were more present after the large influx of immigrants after World Wars I and II.

Tarnegol

Fragment Singing – Call and Response

Tar - ne - gol ____ ku ku ku, Tar - ne - go - let
ku - ku - ri - ku, Kiv - sa ke - ta - na me me me, Pa -
ra ge - do - la ____ moo moo moo ku ku ku ku - ku - ri - ku
me me me ____ moo moo moo   moo moo moo

Teaching Considerations

- Always flip the "r" consonant.
- This song can be used as a Call and Response throughout, or just in the beginning, with the children learning the animal sound responses.
- Add in the rest of the text over several lessons.

Hebrew	English
Tarnegol ku ku ku, *Tahr-neh-gohl koo koo koo*	The rooster says "ku ku ku,"
Tarnegolet kukuriku, *Tahr-neh-gohl-eht koo-koo-ree-koo*	The hen says "kukuriku,"
Kivsa ketana me, me, me, *Keev-suh keh-tah-nah meh meh meh*	The little sheep says "me, me, me,"
Para gedola moo, moo, moo. *Pah-rah guh-doh-lah moo moo moo*	The big cow says "moo, moo, moo."

Ku ku ku
koo koo koo

Kukuriku
koo-koo-ree-koo

Me, me, me
meh, meh, meh

Moo, moo, moo
moo, moo, moo

Music in **Lebanon**

Many musical genres are enjoyed in Lebanon that express the country's Western and Eastern influences, such as Arabic pop, blues, jazz, hip hop, and metal, in addition to classical music and folkloric traditions. The city of Beirut became the cultural capitol for a time after World War II. Folk songs often reflect international influences, and this hybridity has found its way into folk dance traditions as well, such as the *dabke*.

Popular instruments in classical and contemporary music include the *oud* (fretless lute), *mijwiz* (double-reed instrument), *tablah* or *darabouka* (goblet-shaped drum), *daf* or *riq* (small tambourine with drum head), and *buzuq* (long-necked fretted lute akin to the Greek *bouzouki* or Turkish *saz*).

Classical Arabic is spoken throughout the Middle East. However, each region has its own colloquial Arabic. When researching folk songs, it can be difficult to discern country of origin when a language is spoken so broadly. The help of a cultural insider is needed to look for clues within the lyrics, or the dialect, or the pronunciation. In the case of the following song, *Tic Tic Tic Ya'um Sleiman*, Jordanian American pianist and engineer Salam Murtada was able to recognize that the song was in Lebanese Arabic, thereby coming to the logical conclusion that the tune is of Lebanese origin. It is well known throughout Arabic-speaking communities due to the popularity of a famous Lebanese singer known as Fairuz.

Tic Tic Tic Ya'um Sleiman

Movement with the Beat

Songtales

Tic   Tic - i   Tic   ya'___   um   Slei - man.

Tic   Tic - i   Tic   jaw - zik   wane   can

Tic   Tic   Tic   kan   bil___ ha' - alea

am   yek - khowkh   hu   rim - man.

Arabic *(transliterated)*	English
Tic Tici Tic ya' um Sleiman. *tihk tihk-ee tihk yah oom sleigh-man*	Knock knock knock Sleiman's mother.
Tic Tici Tic jawzik wane can? *tihk tihk-ee tihk zhow-zihk wain kan*	Knock knock knock where was your husband?
Tic Tic Tic kan bil ha'alea *tihk tihk tihk kan bi(l) ho(t)-lee*	Knock knock knock he was in the fields
Am yekkhowkh hu rimman. *Ahm yook-tawf-(h)ow (h)oo roo-man*	picking plums and pomegranates.

Movement Instructions

- Motions for the chorus:
  - On *tic tic tic*, children knock on a surface 3 times.
  - On *am yektof khowkh hu rimman*, children reach in the air 4 times alternating hands, on the beat, as if they are picking plums and pomegranates from the trees.

Teaching Considerations

- Sing the "r" consonant lightly flipped.
- Parentheses ( ) around a letter means to listen closely to the recording to hear what happens with the pronunciation.
- ' = glottal stop
- The letter "h" by itself = a whispered "h" sound.
- If an "a" is followed by a consonant (e.g., man, can), these are pronounced with a short "a" vowel.
- If you choose to do the entire song with you singing the verses (creating a Songtale experience), or if you have children in your class who speak colloquial Lebanese Arabic and would like to lead a verse, use the melody and lyrics for the rest of the song found on the next pages.

Tic Tic Tic Ya'um Sleiman (cont.)

Ya sit - ti ya___ sitt b - dour

shou - fi_el - aa - mar keef bi - door

Wa_al na - to - rra___ bid - da shams

wa_al - shams bi - aq - d_el - mar - jan

Verse 1

Ya sitti ya sitt bdour
Yeah siht-tee yeah siht-ihb-doo-er

Oh miss, oh beautiful miss,

Shoufi el-aamar keef bidoor
Shoof-ehl ahm-mer kayf bee-doo-er

Look how the moon spins!

Wa al natorra bidda shams
wehl nah-tooh-ra behd-eh shams

And the sentry, she wants the sun

Wa alshams bi-aqd el-marjan
wihl shams bee-a(kh) dihl mehr-zhan

And the sun is in the coral necklace.

Verse 2

Ammy ya um al-hattab
Ahm-mee yeah ahm-ihl hot-tahb

Oh Uncle, my Uncle the lumberjack

khallina nal'ab al-bab
(kh)ah-lee-nah nihl-ahb ahl-bahb

Let us play on the door!

wa al-jarah bidda am'ha
wihl zhar-ah beh-deh ahm-hah

And the neighbor, she wants wheat

wa al-aamha ind'al-tahhan
wihl ahm-hah ehn-dihl-tah-hahn

And the wheat is at the miller's.

Verse 3

Ya jiddi ya jid el-talj
yeah zhih-dee yeah zhih-deel-tehzh

Oh Grandpa, Oh Grandpa

lihyetak ghattat el-marj
leh-(h)eh-tuhk (h)uh-tuht uhl-muhrzh

your beard covers the meadow

wa al-hawa biddo kheimeh
wehl hah-wah bih-too (kh)ey-mah

and the air wants a tent

wa el-kheimeh bidda kheitan
wehl (kh)ey-mah biht-tuh (kh)ey-than

and the tent needs walls

Verse 4

Weiny al-jimal yahni bi-lqantra
Wayn eel-zhee-mehl yeh-(h) nee bihl-ahn-tah-rah

Where are the camels?
Crouching under the bridge!

shou ta'amnahom qamh wa dura
shoo tah'ahm-nah-(h)ohm ahm (h) wah doo-rah

What do we feed them?
Wheat and corn!

shou sa-aynahom muy mu-attara
shoo sah-ay-ee-nah-hohm my-ee muh uh-tuh-ruh

What do we give them to drink?
Clean water!

ya ammi alghrab jawwizni bintak
yeah ah-mihl-(gh)rahb zhuh-wihz-nee bihn-tehk

Oh my Crow Uncle, marry me to your
   daughter!

Selected Resources for Music from Asia

Recordings

Middle East:

Melodies and Rhythms of Arabic Music. (1981).
    Smithsonian Folkways. https://s.si.edu/303562f
Middle Eastern Songs and Dances for Children.
    Available through www.hinesmusic.com
Piano Music of the Middle East. (1978).
    By Amiram Rigai. https://s.si.edu/2KAhPUU
Travel with Me My Dove and Listen to Me! Songs from the Middle East. (1976.)
    By Margalit Ankory. https://s.si.edu/2N4wedA

Israel:

Yemen: Traditional Music of the North. (1978).
    https://s.si.edu/31F4Erm
Yemenite and Other Israeli Folksongs. (1958).
    By Geula Gill. https://s.si.edu/2N5Iiev

Lebanon:

Lebanon: The Baalbek Folk Festival. (1994).
    By Fairuz. Smithsonian Folkways. https://s.si.edu/2z0LrEe

China:

China: A Musical Anthology of the Orient. (1985).
    UNESCO. https://s.si.edu/33z7Uq3
China: Chuida Wind and Percussive Instrumental Ensembles. (1992).
    UNESCO. https://s.si.edu/2yWozps
Music of China from Smithsonian Folkways (A Playlist). (2014).
    https://s.si.edu/2yVcEbA

Japan:

Japan: Semiclassical and Folk Music. (1974).
    UNESCO. https://s.si.edu/2H935tU
Traditional Folk Dances of Japan. (1959).
    Folkways Records. https://s.si.edu/2Z6cyIK
Traditional Folk Songs of Japan. (1961).
    Smithsonian Folkways. https://s.si.edu/2H3LN1d

Indonesia:

Music of Indonesia (20 volume collection). (1995).
        Smithsonian Folkways Recordings. https://s.si.edu/2MiU7hU

Books

20 Children's Books set in the Middle East and Northern Africa.
    https://bit.ly/303t2mj
Gending Raré: Children's Songs and Games from Bali. (2017).
    By Brent Talbot. GIA Publications, Inc.
Read Globally: 9 Folktales, Fables, and Stories That Introduce Chinese Culture and
History to Kids. https://bit.ly/2H93v3z

Videos

"Rast" by Rahim Alhaj and Souhail Kaspar. (2005).
    https://s.si.edu/2Z8rWrW
Sumunar Minnesota.
    [YouTube Channel]. Features Javanese music and dance.

Convenient links to online resources listed here are also available at GIA Publications
website. Visit www.giamusic.com/firststepsglobal.

North America

TIC OCEAN

Beaufort Sea

Baffin Bay

Dawson

Repulse Bay

Iqaluit

Davis Strait

CANADA

CANADA

Hudson Bay

Edmonton

Vancouver

Winnipeg

Quebec

St. Pierre and Miquelon (FRANCE)

Seattle

Portland

Minneapolis

Toronto

Detroit

Chicago

New York

Washington, D.C.

Denver

UNITED STATES

San Francisco

Dallas

Los Angeles

Bermuda (U.K.)

MEXICO

Gulf of Mexico

Havana

THE BAHAMAS

CUBA

Mexico City

Port-au-Prince

HAITI

DOMINIC REPUBLIC

PUERTO RICO

JAMAICA

Santo Domingo

GUATEMALA

BELIZE

Belmopan

HONDURAS

Tegucigalpa

NICARAGUA

Caribbean Sea

Guatemala

Managua

San Jose

PANAMA

Caracas

TRINIDAD AND TOBAGO

COSTA RICA

Panama

Georget

GUYANA

Bogota

North America

N orth America is the third largest continent by area, and the fourth by population. The 23 independent countries that comprise North America are:

Antigua and Barbuda	Cuba	Haiti	Saint Kitts and Nevis
Bahamas	Dominica	Honduras	Saint Lucia
Barbados	Dominican Republic	Jamaica	Saint Vincent
Belize	El Salvador	Mexico	and the Grenadines
Canada	Grenada	Nicaragua	Trinidad and Tobago
Costa Rica	Guatemala	Panama	United States

Also present are a multitude of island republics governed by other colonizing countries. The list of languages spoken throughout North America is massive and includes, but is not limited to, all First Nation, Native American and indigenous languages, English, French, Spanish, and Portuguese.

Music in **Québec, Canada**

As a large, urban community, Québec is home to a vast range of genres, including jazz, Western classical music, indie folk, and pop styles. Music of First Nations and the Inuit is heard along with immigrant influences, such as Irish tunes, Scottish step dancing, and old French songs. The fiddle is a prominent feature in folk and contemporary music in Québec. Influence from this area followed immigrants into New England in the United States as workers moved to lumberyards and factories.

Allo, Monsieur!

Fragment Singing – Call and Response

A - llo, A - llo, Mon - sieur! Sor - tez vous ce

soir, Mon - sieur. Non, non, Mon - sieur.

Por - quois donc, Mon - sieur? Parce que j'ai le

rheume, Mon - sieur. Tous - sez donc pour voir, Mon -

sieur. A - tchoum! A - tchoum! A - tchoum! A - tchoum!

French	English
Allo, Allo, Monsieur! *Ah-loo, Ah-loo, Meh-syuh*	Hello, hello, sir!
Sortez vous ce soir, Monsieur? *Sohr-teh voo suh swah, Meh-syuh?*	Do you go out tonight, sir?
Non, non, Monsieur. *Noh(n), Noh(n), Meh-syuh*	No, no, sir.
Porquois donc, Monsieur? *Poor-kwah dohnk, Meh-syuh*	Why so, sir?
Parce que j'ai le rheume, Monsieur. *Pahrs-kuh zhey luh ruhm, Meh-syuh*	Because I have a cough, sir.
Toussez donc pour voir, Monsieur. *Too-seh dohnk poor vwa, Meh-syuh*	Cough and be done, sir.
Atchoum! (4x) *Ah-cho*	Achoo!

Teaching Considerations

While chanting, children bounce a ball on beat 1 of each measure. On the word "monsieur," they pass their right leg over the ball.

Trois Canards

Movement for Form and Expression

Trois ca - nards de - ploy - ant leurs ailes coin coin

coin Di - saient a leurs can - nes fi - deles coin coin

coin Quand donc fi - ni - ront nous tour - ments coin coin

coin Quand donc fi - ni - ront nous tour - ments coin

coin coin coin Meu -

nier tu dors, ton mou - lin va trop vi - te Meu -

nier tu dors, ton mou - lin va trop fort.

ton mou - lin ton mou - lin va trop vi - te

ton mou - lin ton mou - lin va trop fort.

French	English
French	**English**
Trois canards deployant leurs ailes *Twa kah-nard day-ploy-aw(n) luh zel*	Three ducks flapping their wings
Coin coin coin *Kwa(n) kwa(n) kwa(n)*	Quack quack quack
Disaient a leurs cannes fideles *Dee-zay(n) tah luhr kah-nay fee-dehl*	Said to their faithful canes
Coin coin coin *Kwa(n) kwa(n) kwa(n)*	Quack quack quack
Quand donc finiront nous tourments? *Kaw(n) daw(n) fee-nee-roh(n) noo toor-maw(n)*	When will our torments end?
Coin coin coin *Kwa(n) kwa(n) kwa(n)*	Quack quack quack
Quand donc finiront nous tourments? *Kaw(n) daw(n) fee-nee-roh(n) noo toor-maw(n)*	When will our torments end?
Coin coin coin coin *Kwa(n) kwa(n) kwa(n) kwa(n)*	Quack quack quack quack

Meunier, tu dors,
Muh-nyay too dor

Miller, you are sleeping,

Ton moulin va trop vite!
Tohn moo-lah(n) vah trohp vee-tuh

Your mill goes too fast!

Meunier, tu dors,
Muh-nyay too dor

Miller, you are sleeping,

Ton moulin va trop fort!
Tohn moo-lah(n) vah trohp for

Your mill goes too strong!

Ton moulin, ton moulin, va trop vite!
Tohn moo-lah(n) tohn moo-lah(n) vah trohp vee-tuh

Your mill goes too fast!

Ton moulin, ton moulin, va trop fort!
Tohn moo-lah(n) tohn moo-lah(n) vah trohp for

Your mill goes too strong!

Movement Instructions

- Start the game with 6 children.
    Group 1 – 3 children
    Group 2 – 3 children
- Form 2 circles, holding hands, with the Group 2 circle in the center and Group 1 holding hands over the hands of Group 2.
- While singing, the children move in a circle.
- Stop at each "coin coin coin," with Group 2 bending the right knee to the floor.
- For the chorus, walk first slowly in a round, and then faster on the words "ton moulin."
- For each additional verse, 2 more children are added (1 for the inner circle and 1 for the outer circle).
- The lyrics then change to match the number of ducks.

4	=	quatre
5	=	cinq
6	=	six
7	=	sept
8	=	huit
9	=	neuf
10	=	dix

(add more if needed)

first steps in global music

Central America

Although Central America is the southernmost area of North America, it is typically discussed as its own region. There are 7 countries in Central America:

Belize   El Salvador   Honduras   Panama
Costa Rica   Guatemala   Nicaragua

Music in **Guatemala**

The marimba has been a popular instrument in Guatemala at least as far back as the seventeenth century, and it is considered to be the national instrument. The Guatemalan marimba was originally constructed from wooden bars with gourd resonators, and eventually evolved to the diatonic scale with a design similar to that used in a Western-style orchestra.

Garifuna music originated in the Caribbean and arrived in Guatemala via residents displaced by the British. Other popular genres include *punta*, and also *chumba* and *hunguhungu*. Western European classical music is found in larger cities and religious institutions, and popular music genres are heard throughout the country. Several genres are popular across Latin America, including reggaetón, salsa, and cumbia, with each being influenced by local traditions to give it a unique Guatemalan flavor.

Arroro

Simple Songs

A la ro - rro ne - ne

A la ro - rro - ro _____

Dor - mi - te mi ni - ño

Dor - mi - te mi a - mor.

Spanish

A la rorro nene, a la rorroro
Ah lah roh-roh* neh-neh

Dormite mi niño
Dohr-mee-teh mee nee-nyoh

Dormite mi amor.
Dohr-mee-teh mee ah-mohr.

English

(soothing sounds – not directly translated)

Go to sleep, my child.

Go to sleep, my love.

Teaching Considerations

- Always flip a single "r" consonant.
- Also flip an "r" at the end of a word.
- Roll the sound whenever there are two "r's" together.

Music in **Mexico**

When thinking of music in Mexico, one of the first genres to come to mind is often *mariachi* from the city of Guadalajara in the Jalisco region. Mariachi music is usually performed with violins, trumpets, guitar, *vihuela* (smaller 5-string guitar), and *guitarron* (bass guitar). The genre of *ranchera* includes songs about love, Mexico, and nature. *Norteño* music utilizes the accordion and the *bajo sexto* (12-string

guitar). *Tejano* music is a blend of Norteño and rock styles from the United States. *Son jarocho* hails from the Veracruz region and often features the *arpa* (harp) and *marimbula* (akin to a thumb piano, but large enough to sit on, and it is plucked acting as the bass voicing). There are many other regional genres, including *son jaliscenses*, *son huasteco*, *son calentano*, and *son michoacano*. Also popular across Mexico are other Latin American dance genres, including mambo, rumba, and cumbia.

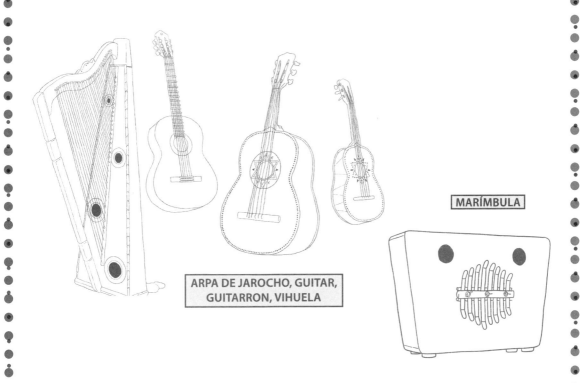

ARPA DE JAROCHO, GUITAR, GUITARRON, VIHUELA

MARÍMBULA

Pin Pin Jarabín

Movement with the Beat

Spanish	English
Pin, pin, Jarabín, *Peen, peen, hah-rah-been*	(no direct translation)
La gallina culeca *Lah gah-yee-nah koo-leh-kah*	The broody hen
Pasó por aquí *Pah-soh pohr ah-kee*	passed by here
Convidando a sus amos *Kohn-vee-dahn-doh ah soos ah-mohs*	inviting her leaders
Y menos a mi. *Ee meh-nohs ah mee*	and less to me.
Cuchara, salero *Koo-chah-rah sah-leh-roh*	Spoon, salt.
Esconde tu dedo *Ehs-kohn-deh too deh-doh*	Hide your finger.

Contextual Considerations

- The translation was at first confusing to me. Dr. Olga Herrera, Mexican American author and English professor, explained some interesting nuances in the text that helped clarify some of the playful feel. She shared that the first line is nonsense and reminds her of other games she played growing up, including "Tin Marin de Don Pingue."
- I was stuck on the word *amos* and why a chicken would have leaders. Dr. Herrera offered, "I think the chicken does have masters, if you think of the chicken as occupying a subservient position in the household (a maid, for example, would refer to her employer as her *ama*). The chicken invites her *amos*, but not the speaker."

Game Instructions

- Children sit in a circle in small groups, 3 or 4 in a group.
- One child is chosen as the *Gallina*, and the others put their hands palms down on the floor or table.
- As the chant is recited, the Gallina touches each child's fingers in order, starting with the pointer finger of her own left hand.
- On the last word – *dedo* – the child whose finger is touched last tucks it under the palm of the hand.
- The Gallina starts again and continues to touch fingers, starting from the next available one.
- The game is over when one person's fingers are completely tucked underneath in one hand. That child becomes the new Gallina and the game begins anew.

The Caribbean

There are 26 independent countries and related territories in the region known as the Caribbean. They include:

Anguilla	Cuba	Martinique	St. Martin
Antigua and Barbuda	Dominica	Montserrat	Saint Vincent
Aruba	Dominican Republic	Dutch Antilles	Trinidad and
Bahamas	Grenada	Puerto Rico	Tobago
Barbados	Guadeloupe	Saint Barthelemy	Turks and Caicos
British Virgin Islands	Haiti	Saint Kitts & Nevis	U.S. Virgin
Cayman Islands	Jamaica	Saint Lucia	Islands

Music in Jamaica

Outside of Jamaica, the most recognizable genre of music is certainly reggae, with Bob Marley as the face of the tradition. Yet, many other important genres exist, including *mento*, *ska*, and *rocksteady* (precursors to reggae), dub music, and dancehall (with its joyful choreography). Mento draws from folk music styles and originated with slaves on the plantations. Ska has rhythm and blues in

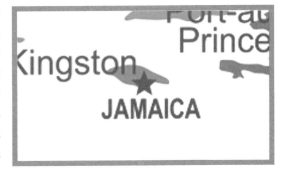

its roots, and it emphasizes the off-beats. Rocksteady developed into a slower groove than Ska, making space for vocalists to join and giving more emphasis to the guitar and electric bass. Children's songs include references to old stories, commercials, internet clips, crisscrossing back and forth across times.

Here Comes Doctor Riding

Simple Songs

Movement with the Beat

Here comes doc - tor rid - ing, rid - ing, rid - ing,

Here comes doc - tor rid - ing, a tee - ly, til - ly, tee - ly.

Here comes doctor riding, riding, riding,
Here comes doctor riding, a teely, tilly, teely.

Verses:

(verse 1)   Solo for doctor

(verse 2)   (group responds) What you riding here for, here for, here for…

(verse 3)   (doctor) Riding for a nurse, a nurse, a nurse…

(verse 4)   (group) Who shall be your nurse, your nurse, your nurse…

(verse 5)   (doctor) _____ shall be my nurse.

Game Instructions

- The doctor stands alone, and the rest of the children are together in a line.
- When the doctor calls a nurse, that child joins the line and becomes the next doctor

Lollipop

Movement with the Beat

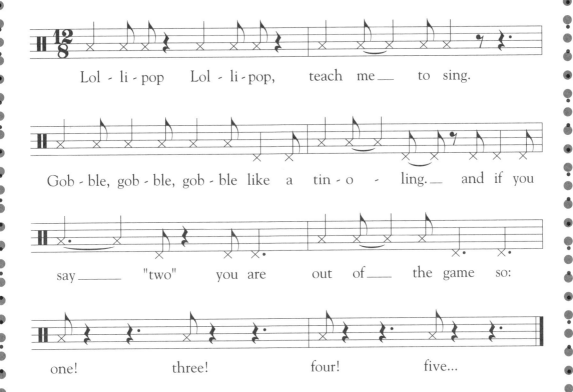

Lol - li - pop   Lol - li - pop,   teach me ___ to sing.

Gob - ble, gob - ble, gob - ble like a   tin - o - ling. ___ and if you

say _____ "two"   you are   out   of ___ the game   so:

one!   three!   four!   five...

Lollipop, lollipop, teach me to sing.
Gobble, gobble, gobble like a tin-o-ling.
And if you say "two" you are out of the game,
So: One! Three! Four! Five!...

Game Instructions

- The leader calls out a number from 1 to 9 in measure 5.
- After the word "so," the children begin to count with one child at a time calling out the next number, skipping any number that contains the leader's number until someone misses or makes a mistake. (For example, if the leader calls out "2," then the children need to skip calling out 12, and any of the 20s, and so on.)
- Once someone misses, that child is out of the counting and can keep a beat with his or her hands, or with rhythm sticks, so as not to make this an elimination game if so desired.

Music in **Puerto Rico**

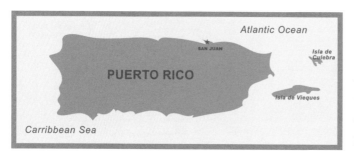

Puerto Rico is a territory of the United States, and Puerto Ricans are U.S. citizens. The island has three important cultural and ethnic influences: Spanish from colonization, West African from slaves, and Taíno (indigenous). By 1850, half of all Puerto Ricans were combinations of African and Spanish backgrounds.

Two well-known folkloric traditions are *plena* and *bomba*. In bomba, the *barriles* (barrel-like drums) and perhaps a *cua* are featured. In plena, *panderetas* (hand drums) and guiro are featured, often alongside a full band that may include the *cuatro* (guitar-like instrument). Both genres are sources of political and spiritual expression. The lyrics express frustration and sadness over conditions, and the songs were often used as a form of rebellion. After the devastating hurricanes that hit the island in 2017, these genres were a source of strength and comfort, bringing people together through music while the community was brought back to life.

PANDERETA

BARRILES

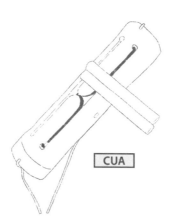

CUA

CUATRO

El Coquí

Movement for Form and Expression

El co - quí, El co - quí a mi me en - can - ta,

Es tan lin-do el can - tar del co - quí_____ Por las

no-ches al ir a - cos - tar-me me a-dor me-ce can -

tan-do a - sí_____ Co - quí, co - quí, co - quí quí quí

quí, Co - quí, co - quí, co - quí quí quí quí

Spanish	English
El coquí, el coquí a mi me encanta.	I love the frog.
El koh-kee, el-koh-keeah mee mehn-kahn-tah	
Es tan lindo el cantar del coquí.	It is so pretty when it sings "coqui."
Ehs tahn leen-doh el kahn-tar del koh-kee	
Por las noches al ir acostarme,	At night when going to bed,
Por las noh-chehs ahl eer ah-kohs-tar-meh	
Me ador mece cantando así.	I'm rocked to sleep singing like this...
Meh-ah-dor meh-seh kahn-tahn-doh ah-see.	
Coquí, coquí, coquí quí quí quí (2x)	
Koh-kee...	

Teaching Considerations

- Bring the children in on the "coqui's" first after they have identified when and how many.
- Emphasize the feel of 3/4 by alternating tapping groupings of 3 (on one side, then the other side).
- Using a frog puppet, one child sings the ending "coquis" as a solo while moving the frog on beat 1.

Music in **Cuba**

It has been said that Cuba has had a greater influence on popular music and dance traditions worldwide than any other country in Latin America, and perhaps beyond. The list of unique traditions that emerged from the culture of West African and Spanish practices gave us rumba, guaganco, son, guajira, mambo, cha-cha-cha, to name only a few. Hybridity is a regular feature in Cuban music, also referred to as *syncretism*—the fusing together of different cultures (or religions), in many cases along with Western classical music and dance traditions. It is difficult to find traces of indigenous practices in Cuban music today, as much of the culture did not survive the arrival of European colonizers. For example, one can hear Spanish-style guitars alongside West African-style percussion, including congas, claves, and maracas. *Bata* (drums) are used in the music of Santeria, a religion combining Christian practices with West African religious rituals and deities. Cajons are played for rumba, perhaps along with *marimbulas* (large plucked box). The holiday of Carnival is celebrated across the country with children of all ages singing, playing, and dancing in the parades, from smaller villages to large city festivals.

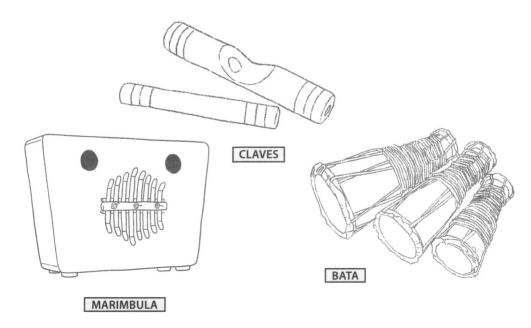

CLAVES

BATA

MARIMBULA

Pico y Pala

Fragment Singing
Songtales

pu cha cha Lo-co-mo-to-ra don-de tu vas?— Yo

voy a cua-tro ca-mi-nos, Son-go La Ma-

1.
- ya y vi-ro pa tras— Pum

2.
- ya y vi-ro pa tras—

Gua - oo Gua - oo

Gua-oo Gua-oo Gua-oo Gua-oo Gua - oo

Spanish	English
Guaoo Guaoo *Gwah-ooh*	(train sounds)
Pico y pala, pico y pala, pico y pala, compañero, *Pee-kee pah-lah kohm-pah nyeh-roh*	Pick and shovel, friend,
Pico y pala, pico y pala, pico y pala, soy central. *Pee-kee-pah-la soy sehn-trahl*	I am to the station.
Pumpu cha cha pumpu cha cha *Poom-poo chah chah*	(train sounds)
Locomotora donde tu vas? *Loh-koh-moh-toh-tah dohn-deh too vahs*	Where are you going, train?
Yo voy a cuatro caminos, *Yoh voy ah kwa-troh kah-mee-nohs*	I go four ways,
Songo la maya y viro pa tras. *Sohn-goh la mah-yah-ee vee-roh pah trahs*	Songo, La Maya, and then I return.

Teaching Considerations

- This tune has opportunities to create a call and response in different ways: children sing "Pico y Pala," and you sing the rest, add "Gua-oo," or/and add "pum pum, cha cha."
- Layer in the rest of the words over multiple classes.
- Add simple percussion accompaniments using maracas (or smaller shakers) or drums (from the children or from you playing something a bit more sophisticated), or create an internal section of measures that allows for free play while you hold down the steady beat or groove.

Music in **Haiti**

Music in Haiti reflects many influences from groups that have settled on the island, direct neighbor to the Dominican Republic. West African sounds mix with French and Spanish elements as well as Taíno (indigenous) influences, though to a lesser degree. Church hymns are heard alongside pop songs (including the local genres *vodou*, *kompa*, and *mizik rasin*), hip hop tunes, blues, jazz, and religious music associated with holidays. As in Brazil and Cuba, Carnival is an important religious celebration in Haiti along with its attendant music and dance festivities.

Folk music includes work songs, social celebrations, and ritual drumming and chants. There are several Haitian genres of folk music and dance, including *Affranchi* (The Colonial Dance), *Kontradans* (Haitian Contra Dancing), *Méringue* (The Whipped-Egg Dance), and *Rara* (Easter Voodoo Music).

Toi Si Bonne

Movement with the Beat

	French		English

French

Toi si bonne, toi si parfaite,
Twah see buhn-uh, twah see par-feh-tuh

qui nous aime de son amour,
kee nooz eh-meh duh sohn ah-moor

Maman, c'est aujourd' hui ta fete.
Mah-mah(n) set oh-zhor-dwee tah feht

Pour tes enfants quell heureux jour.
Poor tehz ahn-fahn kehl ehr-uh zhoor.

English

You, so good, you, so perfect,

who loves us with your love,

Mom, today is your party.

For your children, what a happy day.

Teaching Considerations

- Some settings allow for the recognition of a birthday. It could be interesting to have a collection of birthday tunes and a child can select the music culture with which to be celebrated.
- Use the song as an A section, with many possibilities for extension with B sections. Try instruments, or movement while you accompany, or create a longways set (or other formation—change it up on each repeat of the B) and ask the children to choreograph a set of movements.
- Have the children work with a partner or larger group to create hand movements (clapping patterns, etc.) to accompany the song.

Selected Resources for Music from North America

Recordings

Canada:

Canada: Inuit Games and Songs. (1976).
    UNESCO. https://s.si.edu/2Z4k2Qz
Folk Songs of France and French Canada. (1957).
    By Jacques Labrecque. Folkways Records. https://s.si.edu/33DCXBl
Game Songs of French Canada. (1956).
    Folkways Records. https://s.si.edu/2H4Yt8a
Songs of French Canada. (1955).
    By Hélène Baillargeon and Alan Mills. Folkways Records. https://s.si.edu/301hhgd

CENTRAL AMERICA

Guatemala:

Chapinlandia – Marimba Music of Guatemala. (2007).
    Smithsonian Folkways Recordings. https://s.si.edu/33zv6Vm
Music of Guatemala (Volumes 1 & 2). (1969).
    Folkways Records. https://s.si.edu/2TvobaY

Mexico:

Mariachi Music of Mexico. (1954).
    Cook Records. https://s.si.edu/2TvQBl4

CARIBBEAN

Puerto Rico:

Para Todos Ustedes. (2005).
    By Los Pleneros de la 21. Smithsonian Folkways Records. https://s.si.edu/2KyQt1h
Puerto Rico in Washington. (1996).
    By Marcial Reues y sus Pleneros and Cuerdas De Borinquen. Smithsonian Folkways Recordings. https://s.si.edu/2KARpSZ

Cuba:

Café Cubano. (2008).
Putumayo Records.
Folk Music of Cuba. (1995).
UNESCO. https://s.si.edu/2yX9Eve
Sacred Rhythms of Cuban Santería. (1995).
Smithsonian Folkways Recordings. https://s.si.edu/2OV9dfO

Haiti:

Music of Haiti: Vol. 1, Folk Music of Haiti. (1951).
Folkways Records. https://s.si.edu/2yYaDeu

Books/Articles

Tito Matos: Puerto Rican plena drummer.
https://s.si.edu/2KzgIox
Los Pleneros de la 21: Afro-Puerto Rican traditions.
https://s.si.edu/2yYaBmS

Videos

Carlos Mejía Discusses Marimba Traditions. (2006).
https://s.si.edu/2TvQBl4
Fandango-Bombazo (Puerto Rican Jam Session) at 2006 Smithsonian Folklife
Festival. (2006). https://s.si.edu/2TyL79k
"La Bamba" by José Gutiérrez and Los Hermanos Ochoa from *La Bamba: Sones
Jarochos from Veracruz.* (2005). https://s.si.edu/2YVpS7L
"Mexico Lindo" by Natividad "Nati" Cano from *Llegaron Los Camperos!: Nati
Cano's Mariachi.* (2005). https://s.si.edu/301g8oI

*Convenient links to online resources listed here are also available at GIA Publications
website. Visit www.giamusic.com/firststepsglobal.*

Caribbean Sea

Caracas

TRINIDAD AND
TOBAGO

VENEZUELA

Georgetown

Bogota

GUYANA

Paramaribo

COLOMBIA

French Guiana
(FRANCE)

SURINAME

Quito

ECUADOR

Manaus

PERU

B R A Z I L

Lima

BRAZIL

La Paz

Brasilia

BOLIVIA

PARAGUAY

Sao
Paolo

Asuncion

*Archipelago
Juan Fernandez
(CHILE)*

Cordoba

URUGUAY

Santiago

Buenos Aires

Montevideo

ARGENTINA

Bahia Blanca

CHILE

*Falkland Islands
(Islas Malvinas)*

*South Georgia and
South Sandwich Islands*

South America

South America is the fourth largest continent. In addition to the French Guiana there are 12 independent countries:

Argentina	Chile	Guyana	Suriname
Bolivia	Colombia	Paraguay	Uruguay
Brazil	Ecuador	Peru	Venezuela

Music in Brazil

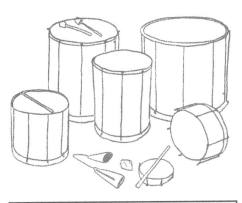

(CLOCKWISE FROM LOWER LEFT)
REPENIQUE, SURDO (3 DIFFERENT SIZES),
CAXIXI, TAMBORIM, AGOGO BELL.

Brazil is vast geographic area with diverse terrain and culture. Indigenous groups number over 100, West African practices are still vibrant in places, and Portuguese influence abounds. There are so many genres unique to Brazil, including *bossa nova* (meaning "new trend"—featured bass, guitar, drums, piano and voice), *choro* (instrumental music), *axé* (West African origins) and, of course, *samba*. Samba schools are found throughout Brazil and spend much of the year preparing elaborate costuming, and music and dance performances for the Carnival. The larger cities such as Rio de Janeiro hold Carnival celebrations that feature performing groups with thousands of members. The *batería* (battery) is the percussion section of such a group and can feature anywhere from a small number of players up to several hundred processing through the streets. The instruments include several drums (*repenique, caxixi, surdo, tamborim*), bells (*agogo*), and other metal shakers (*ganza, chocalho*) and noisemakers of assorted types (*apito, reco reco, cuíca*).

Ó Embolcé

Fragment Singing
Movement for Form and Expression
Movement with the Beat

Ó_____ em - bo-lé‿em bo - leé_____ Ó__

__ em - bo-lé‿em - bo - lá_____ Ó_____

__ em - bo-lé‿em bo - leé_____ Ó_____

__ em - bo-lé‿em - bo - lá_____ Em-bo - la

pai, em-bo-la mãe, em-bo-la fil-ha, Eu tam-bém sou da fa-

mi - lia Eu tam-bém que-ro‿em-bo - la Ó_____

__ em - bo-lé‿em bo - leé_____ Ó__

__ em - bo-lé‿em - bo - lá_____ Ó__

Contextual Considerations

- *Embolada* is a genre of music from the northeast region of Brazil.
- *Embole*, *emboleé*, and *embola* are all plays on that word and mean to dance and perform the Embolada.
- The lyrics in Embolada are often humorous, or they contain words that are linked by their sound rather than definition, as seen here with "cinco ripa, bota pipa."
- Embolá and pingá in their formal Portuguese forms are *embolar* and *pingar*. These "á" verb forms are widely used in popular music.

Teaching Considerations

- Have the children play simple rhythms or steady beat on instruments from Brazil. The ones listed here are specific for samba, but there are a wide range of Brazilian percussion instruments available.

Brazilian Portuguese	English
Ó embolé emboleé, ó embolé embolá (2x) *oh ehm-boh-lehm boh-lay, oh ehm-boh-lehm-boh-lah*	(see below for explanation)
Embola pai, embola mãe, *ehm-boh-luh pah-ee, ehm-boh-luh muh-ee* Embola filha, *ehm-boh-la fee-lee-yah*	This refers to taking turns creating rhymes – Dad's turn (pai), Mom's (mai), daughter's (filha)
Eu também sou da familia *Eh-oo tahm-behm soh dah fah-mee-lee-yah*	I am also from the family.
Eu também quero embolá *Eh-oo tahm-behm ehm-boh-lah*	I want to embolá, too.
Cinco Filipa, cinco pipa *seen-koh fee-lee-pah, seen-koh pee-pah*	Five (word that rhymes), five kites,
Cinco ripa, bota pipa *seen-koh (h)ee-pah, boh-tah pee-pah**	Five boards, boot kite.
Dentro o piri *dehn-chroh pee-ree*	Put the kite inside the piri (maybe a bowl or sink)
Para o piri não pinga *pah-rah pee-ree noh peen-gah*	So that it doesn't drip.

*(the "h" sound is a bit rough, toward a throaty "ch")

Music in **Peru**

Music in Peru draws on influences from Andean, Spanish, and West African cultural practices. Afro-Peruvian music was developed by West African slaves in western Peru. Singing can be accompanied by a *quijada de burro* (a donkey jawbone), *cajita* (a small wooden box that can be struck on the top and side, and the lid can be tapped open and closed), and *cajon* (box drum) and other drums.

Indigenous culture is thriving, and old dances with live music can be seen in parades connected with the many religious feast days and rituals. Panpipes and *charango* (small, plucked lute-like instrument) are popular in Andean music, and there are other types of single flutes used as solo instruments or to accompany dance and songs. Also well loved in Andean culture is the several centuries old *huayno* music and dancing, still heard and seen at some weddings.

Ferrocarril

Movement with the Beat

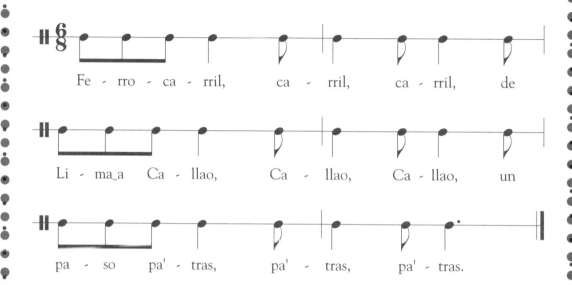

Fe - rro - ca - rril, ca - rril, ca - rril, de

Li - ma_a Ca - llao, Ca - llao, Ca - llao, un

pa - so pa' - tras, pa' - tras, pa' - tras.

Spanish	English
Ferrocarril, carril, carril,	A little train, train, train,
Feh-roh-kah-reel	
de Lima a Callao, Callao, Callao,	From Lima to Callao, Callao, Callao,
day Lee-mah Kah-yaow	
un paso pa'tras,	One step back,
oon pah-soh pah-trahs	
pa'tras, pa'tras.	Back, back.
pah-tras, pah-tras	

Teaching Considerations

- All single "r" consonants are flipped.
- All double "r" consonants are rolled.

Game Instructions

- The song can be sung in a circle holding hands, or by reaching around to hold hands behind the back of the neighbor, or in a line lightly touching the shoulders of the child in front.
- Step forward 8 steps (see below), and then jump back 4 steps. Play with the speed of the song for fun.

Jumping forward:	Jumping back:
1 Ferro	1 un paso
2 carril	2 pa' tras
3 carril	3 pa' tras
4 carril	4 pa' tras
5 de Lima	
6 a Callao	
7 Callao	
8 Callao	

Music in **Chile**

As in so many countries, Chilean music features many sounds to form a national identity. These include folkloric genres such as *cueca*, *bolero*, and *cumbia* alongside hip hop, rock, and pop. Chile's folk music is broadly organized into 3 regions with unique sounds and stylings: northern, central, and southern. Cueca is known as the national dance in Chile and has variations by region. Chilean youth have created a new version (known as *Cueca Brava*) that has moved it away from its old traditions, as so often happens with the artistic practices of youths.

Strummed and plucked string instruments are prominent in Chile, including the *charango* (small lute-like instrument), *guitarron Chileno* (like a smaller guitar with 25 strings), and *tiple* (12-stringed instrument similar to the guitarron). The guitar and accordion are often heard in Southern Chile, while in other regions one can hear cow-horn trumpets, snare drums, and indigenous wooden flutes, such as the *kultrun*, *trutruka*, and *trompe*.

Caballo Blanco

Songtales

Es mi ca - ba - llo blan - co,

co - mo_el a - ma - ne - cer.

Siem - pre jun - ti - tos va - mos.

Es mi_a - mi - go más bien. Mi ca -

ba - llo, mi ca - ba - llo ga - lo -

pan - do va. Mi ca - ba - llo, mi ca -

ba - llo, que se va_y se va!

Spanish	English
Es mi caballo blanco *Ehs mee kah-bah-yoh blahn-koh*	My horse is white
como el amanecer *Koh-moh-el ah-mah-neh-sehr*	like the dawn.
Siempre juntitos vamos, *See-ehm-preh hoon-tee-tohs vah-mohs*	We always go together.
Es mi amigo más bien. *Ehs mee-ah mee-goh mahs byehn*	He is my best friend.
Mi caballo, mi caballo *Mee kah-bah-yoh*	My horse, my horse
galopando va. *gah-loh-pahn-doh vah*	goes galloping.
Mi caballo, mi caballo, *Mee kah-bah-yoh*	My horse, my horse
qué va y se va! *Kay vah-ee seh vah*	just keeps going on and on!

Teaching Considerations

- The last 8 measures are a good starting point to have the children responding.
- The children could start with only the words "mi caballo" and then add the rest of those two phrases as they seem ready after multiple hearings.
- This song presents an easy opportunity to include the children in creating more verses about the wonderful caballo, whether in Spanish, English, or another language!
- Use children's artwork to help create verses.
- Scan the children's artwork to make a digital songbook to send home for families to share together, or post online for easy access from home.

Selected Resources for Music from South America

Recordings

Brazil:
Brazil: Songs of Protest.
    Monitor Records. https://s.si.edu/2Z8xKhr
Music of Brazil from Smithsonian Folkways Playlist. (2014).
    https://s.si.edu/2Z0JOoN
Songs & Dances of Brazil. (1956).
    Folkways Records. https://s.si.edu/2ORZU02

Peru:
Music of Peru from Smithsonian Folkways Playlist. (2015).
    https://s.si.edu/2sQLvUt
Traditional Music of Peru Series (8 Volumes). (2002).
    Smithsonian Folkways. https://s.si.edu/2TvWVsZ

Chile:
Chile: Hispano-Chilean Metisse Traditional Music. (1988).
    UNESCO. https://s.si.edu/2TyjgWY
Que Viva el Canto! Songs of Chile. (2008). By Rafael Manríquez.
    Smithsonian Folkways Records. https://s.si.edu/2N4nHHA

Books/Articles

Black Rhythms of Peru: Reviving African Musical Heritage in the Black Pacific. (2006).
    By Heidi Carolyn Feldman. Middletown, CT: Wesleyan University Press.
Culture and Customs of Chile. (2000).
    By Guillermo Castillo-Feliú. Westport, CT: Greenwood Press.
Luiz Bonfá: Brazilian Bossa Nova Guitarist.
    https://s.si.edu/2OYugy2
Music in Brazil: Experiencing Music, Expressing Culture. (2006).
    By John Patrick Murphy. New York: Oxford Music Press.
The Music of Brazil. (1989).
    By David Appleby. University of Texas Press.

Videos

A Taste of Afro-Peruvian Music. (Dec. 22, 2016).
   By Tony Succar. https://youtu.be/keboPv6ZAvE
Chilean traditional folk dance: Huasos. (Jul 14 2011).
   https://youtu.be/AjJu9Q4yVJ8
 "The Great Inka Road" Family Day 6 – Peruvian Music & Dance. (Sept 17, 2015).
   https://youtu.be/l3uGyJ3JHn0

Convenient links to online resources listed here are also available at GIA Publications website. Visit www.giamusic.com/firststepsglobal.

MUSIC FROM
Europe

Jan Mayen
(NORWAY)

miit

*Norwegian
Sea*

SWEDEN

FINLAND

Murmansk

NORWAY

Helsinki

Oslo

Tallinn

Stockholm

EST.

Saint
Petersburg

Riga

LAT.

Mosco

*North
Sea*

DENMARK

LITHUANIA

LITH.

Vilnius

UNITED

Copenhagen

RUS.

BELARUS

Dublin

Amsterdam

Berlin

Warsaw

IRELAND

KINGDOM

NETH.

POLAND

Kyiv

Brussels

GERMANY

BEL.

Prague

London

LUX.

CZ. REP.

UKRAINE

Kharkiv

Munich

Vienna

SLOV.

MOLDOVA

Donetsk

Paris

AUS.

Budapest

FRANCE

SWITZ.

HUNG.

ROMANIA

Bordeaux

Milan

SLO.

Belgrade

Bucharest

CRO.

BOS.&
HER.

Black Sea

Monaco

ITALY

SER.

BULGARIA

GEORGIA

Barcelona

MONT.

Istanbul

PORTUGAL

Rome

MACE.

ALB.

Ankara

AF

SPAIN

GREECE

TURKEY

Lisbon

Malaga

Tunis

Athens

Europe

There are 44 countries in Europe. The following is a list of countries:

Albania	Finland	Luxembourg	Russia*
Andorra	France	Malta	San Marino
Austria	Germany	Moldova	Serbia
Belarus	Greece	Monaco	Slovakia
Belgium	Hungary	Montenegro	Slovenia
Bosnia & Herzegovina	Iceland	Netherlands	Spain
Bulgaria	Ireland	North Macedonia	Sweden
Croatia	Italy	Norway	Switzerland
Czech Republic	Latvia	Poland	Ukraine
Denmark	Liechtenstein	Portugal	United Kingdom
Estonia	Lithuania	Romania	Vatican City

* technically in both Europe and Asia

These borders, as in so many places in the world, have shifted over the centuries, and neighboring countries share many commonalities alongside cultural differences. Geographical features such as mountain ranges and oceans create barriers to the transmission of cultural practices, and they can create unique pockets of music.

Music in **Lithuania**

Lithuania is one of the three Baltic countries, or Baltic states, including Latvia and Estonia. It is the southernmost of the three regions and is bordered by Poland, Latvia, and Belarus. Pop music has a large audience, and this is what is most-oft heard on radio stations, with the Eurovision Song Contest as the culminating annual event. Summer music festivals are hugely popular  and are typically held in the countryside in beautiful venues. Some of the festivals include:

> *Mėnuo juodaragis* (neo-folk and neo-pagan music)
> *Galapagai* (rock)
> *Visagino kantri* (country music)
> *Tamsta muzika* (indie-type music)
> *Yaga* (reggae, dub, electronica)
> *Akaciju alėja* (sung poetry)

UNESCO also recognized the song festival known as *Dainu šventė*, and in 2003 recognized the massive Baltic song and dance celebrations held every fifth year in Estonia and Latvia, and every fourth year in Lithuania. These multi-day events bring together as many as 40,000 singers and dancers.

Lithuania's polyphonic singing tradition of *Sutartinės* (from the word for "in concordance") is traditionally performed by female singers from the northeastern part of the country. Men sometimes perform instrumental versions using panpipes, horns, and wooden trumpets. There are more than 40 different styles of performing Sutartinės. In 2010, UNESCO identified the tradition as an Intangible Cultural Heritage. The genre was recognized for its importance in promoting cultural values and identity. Following is a sutartinės simple enough for younger children.

Sutartinės

Simple Songs

Lithuanian	English
Kai mes buvom dalilio *Kah-ee mehs boo-vohm dah-lee-loh*	When we were living
Trys sesutės, dalilio *Trees seh-soo-tehs dah-lee-loh*	three sisters together
Mes turėjom dalilio *Mehs tuh-reh-yohm dah-lee-loh*	We had
po darželį, dalilio *poh dahr-zheh-lee dah-lee-loh*	each a flower garden.
Vienam darže dalilio *Vee-nahm dahr-zheh dah-lee-loh*	In one garden
baltos rožės dalilio *Bahl-tohs roh-zhes dah-lee-loh*	there were white roses.
Antram darže dalilio *Ahn-trahm dahr-zheh dah-lee-loh*	In the second
Žalios rūtos dalilio *Zhah-lyohs roo-tohs dah-lee-loh*	green rue flowers
Trečiam darže dalilio *Treh-chee-ahm dahr-zheh dah-lee-loh*	And in the third,
Diemedėlis dalilio. *Dee-meh-day-lees dah-lee-loh*	Lady's flowers of love.

Contextual Considerations

- All "r" consonants are lightly flipped.
- There are various genres of Sutartinės, including work songs, season songs, or holiday songs.
- With short melodies and only two to five pitches, all three parts together create an interesting dissonance.
- This particular tune is a *trejinės*, meaning three singers sing the same melody and lyrics in canon.

Teaching Considerations

- When first introducing the song, it can work as a call and response, with the children responding on some of the "dalilo" occurrences.
- Add more as the children grow in their comfort over multiple lessons. This type of approach allows for multiple hearings of the words (and opportunities for you to keep it fresh in your mind and on your tongue).
- Although typically performed in parts, the tune is certainly simple enough to learn in unison. Perhaps the children can perform in canon with you! Or if you have started to introduce simple rounds, this one just may work out.
- If singing in unison, find quality recordings for the children to hear (e.g., on the UNESCO site listed in the resources at the end of the Europe section).

Music in **Bulgaria**

Bulgarian society includes western classical music, eastern-influenced pop styles, Arabic flavors, and more. In terms of folkloric traditions, the country is divided into several regions, each with its own unique music, dance, instrument techniques, and even embroidery and costuming particular to certain areas.

The songs of the Šop (Sofia, the capital city) region are typically work songs, story songs, and ballads. What is sometimes heard as dissonant to an outsider is prevalent throughout this region. Singers often split into a drone part and a melody part. The drone may move back and forth between two neighboring pitches. This creates intense combinations between the two melodies with regular sustained seconds and other tense intervals that resolve beautifully.

The Northern region has a long history of songs connected to work and rituals, harvest and animals, and marriage and war. The *Dobrudja* area in the northeast of Bulgaria features songs that combine male and female voices, and songs to pass the time while doing chores (such as quilting, weaving, and sewing).

From *Thrace* come the songs most shared throughout the world. There are highly ornamented slow songs for celebrations, with a particular "wedding" style of singing that is highly regarded. The Bulgarian bagpipe (gajda) is featured prominently here. The folk dances from this region are some of the most popular around the world. The *kaval* (end-blown flute), *gajda*, *gajdulka* (reed instrument), and *tupan* (bass drum played on both sides) are heavily featured in Thracian music.

The *Pirin* region features more percussion than other regions and includes *tamburas* (strummed/plucked lute-like instruments), while the *Rhodope* region is known for its music. After all, the legend says the mythical singer, Orpheus (with his lute), was born in the forests of Rhodope. The song *Izlel delio e haidutin* is included on the Voyager recording and will be playing in space for the next 60,000 years.

GAJDULKA, BOUZOUKI, GAJDA, TAMBURA,
RIQ, ZURLA, TUPAN, DVOYANKA, DOUMBEK

Moe Munečko Kokiče

Songtales

Mo - e mu - ni - čko ko-ki - če stun - ko ne - žno
stu - bul - tse, što do-šlo si tol - koz ra - no
sam sa-mo, sa - mi - čko? što do-šlo si
tol - koz ra - no sam sa-mo, sa - mi - čko.

Bulgarian (transliterated from Cyrillic alphabet)	English
(Verse 1 – the child) Moe muničko kokiče *Moh-eh muh-nee-chkoh koh-kee-cheh*	My little snow flower
stunko nežno stubultse, *stuhn-koh nezh-noh stuh-buhl-tseh*	with a thin, delicate stem.
što došlo si tolkoz rano *Shto doh-shloh see tohl-kohz rah-noh*	why did you come so early
Sam samo, samičko? *Sahm sah-moh, sah-mee-chkoh*	All alone?
(Verse 2 – the flower) Az došlo sum tuk detentse *Ahz-doh-shlo soom tuhk deh-tehn-tseh*	I've come here, little child,
Radost da vi izvestya, *Rah-dohst dah vee eez-vehs-tyah*	to bring the happy news
Če taz zima si otiva *Cheh tah zee-mah see oh-tee-vah*	that the winter is leaving
i pristiga proletta. *ee pree-stee-gah proh-leh-tah*	and the spring is coming.

Teaching Considerations

- The lyrics are a conversation between a flower and the child. You can be one part, and the children the other, or you can split the lines up among small groups.
- This song can be taught in small pieces over multiple lessons to slowly catch the Bulgarian words.

Music in **Poland**

Music in Poland reflects a strong western classical tradition through composers such as Chopin and Górecki. Pop music genres are heard along with jazz, pop, rock, and folkloric styles. Many of the most familiar dance genres heard in western classical music originated in Poland, including the mazurka, polonaise, and *krakowiak* (partner dance). Unfortunately, a large amount of materials related to Polish folk music was taken or destroyed during World War II. The Polish community worked endlessly to try and piece back together the cultural heritage that was so grievously damaged during the Nazi occupation. The town of Zakopane has hosted an annual International Festival of Highland Folklore for more than 50 years, attracting attendants from around Poland and abroad.

Dobry Wieczór Wam

Movement with the Beat

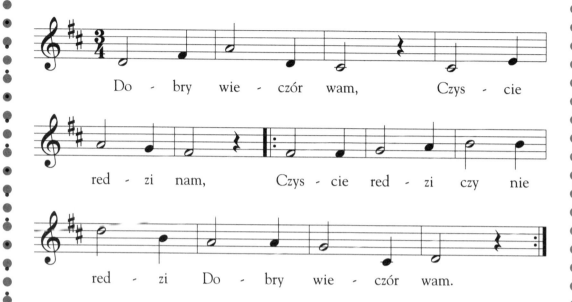

Do - bry wie - czór wam, Czys - cie

red - zi nam, Czys - cie red - zi czy nie

red - zi Do - bry wie - czór wam.

Teaching Considerations

- This tune seems meant for an end-of-year celebration, or a farewell to a fellow student or staff member, or for any sort of send-off.
- As there are far fewer words than it may appear at first, the whole song is certainly accessible for children.
- Add in older children on a descant with voices, or recorders, or glockenspiels, etc.

Polish	English
Dobry wieczór wam *Daw-brih veh-chohr vahm*	Good evening to you,
Czyscie redzi nam *Chih-sheh red-zee nahm*	Whether you know us,
//Czyscie redzi, czy nie redzi *Chih-sheh red-zee, chih neh red-zee*	Whether you know us, whether you don't
Dobry wieczór wam// *Daw-brih veh-chohr vahm*	Good evening to you.
Dobry wieczór wam *Daw-brih veh-chohr vahm*	Good evening to you.
Zaśpiewamy wam *Zah-shpeh-vah-mih vahm*	We will sing to you.
//Czyście redzi, czy nie redzi *Chih-sheh red-zee, chih neh red-zee*	Whether you like it, whether you don't.
Zaśpiewamy wam// *Zah-shpeh-vah-mih vahm*	We will sing to you.

Music in the **Republic of Georgia**

The country of Georgia sits in Eurasia—partly in Europe and partly in Asia. It is bordered by Armenia, Azerbaijan, and Russia, and has some of the oldest documented singing traditions.

Georgian music is widely recognized for its rich and old tradition of polyphony. There are many regional styles of vocal polyphony, all falling within either "eastern" or "western" traditions. From the eastern traditions are several regions, including Kartli-Kakheti and Meskheti. *Supra* (songs sung at the banquet table) showcase a continuous droning bass with dueting soloists singing melodies. A particular song-style from this region known as *Chakrulo* was included on the Golden Record on the Voyager spaceship in 1977 (along with the Bulgarian tune from the Rhodope region). The western traditions include the following regions: Imereti, three in the Caucasus mountains (Svaneti, Racha, and Lechkhumi), and three along the coast of the Black Sea (Samegrelo, Guria, and Achara). In 2001, UNESCO recognized Georgian polyphonic singing as an Intagible Cultural Heritage of Humanity, working to ensure the preservation of the traditions.

Iavnana

Simple Songs

I - av - na - na_____ bat' - o - ne -

bo var - do bat' - o - ne - bo

Dat' - k'bit, dat' - k'bit, da sho - shi - mindt,

var - do bat' - o - ne - bo

Georgian (transliterated)	English
Iavnana, bat'onebo, vardo bat'onebo *Ee-ahv-nah-nah, baht-oh-neh-boh,* *Vahr-doh baht-oh-neh-boh*	Lullaby, violet, oh spirits, oh rose, oh spirits
Dat'k'bit, dat'k'bit, da shoshimindt, *Daht-kbeet, daht-kbeet, dah shoh-shee-meendt*	Enjoy, enjoy, oh rose
vardo bat'onebo *vahr-doh baht-oh-neh-boh*	oh spirits

Contextual Considerations

- The title *Iavnana* refers to an old form of lullaby often used when a child is sick. Some songs used for healing address the "batonebi" (the spirits believed to have made the child sick).
- This particular Iavnana is from the Racha region of Georgia.

Teaching Considerations

- As the song is slow and spare, any extensions would likely have the same tone.
- Ask the children to show how they might move while singing. Play with the division of the beat—walk on the half note (describing it in whatever way meets where the children are with music labels), walk on the quarter note, tip toe on the eighth notes, and so on.
- Play finger cymbals ever so lightly on the rests.

Selected Resources for Music from Europe

Recordings

Lithuania/Baltics:

Lithuanian Folk Songs in the United States. (1955).
   Folkways Records. https://s.si.edu/2KJ90a8
Lithuanian Songs and Dances.
   Monitor Records. https://s.si.edu/303R54j
Songs of Amber. (1990). By Amber. Mickey Hart Collection.
https://s.si.edu/33xU0Vd

Bulgaria:

Bulgaria: Musics and Musicians of the World. (1983).
   UNESCO. https://s.si.edu/2YPdohJ
Koutev Bulgarian National Ensemble.
   Monitor Records. https://s.si.edu/2KAHvAU

Poland:

Memories of Poland.
   By Bolek Zawadski. Monitor Records. https://s.si.edu/2yXTPo3
Polish Folk Songs and Dances. (1954).
   Folkways Records. https://s.si.edu/2MjSiRO
The Polish State Folk Ballet "Slask": The Silesian Song and Dance Ensemble. (1996).
   Monitor Records. https://s.si.edu/31AnL5O

Books/Articles

Georgian polyphonic singing.
   https://bit.ly/2sAWiS1
Sutartinės, Lithuanian multipart songs.
   https://bit.ly/2AuCsPn

Videos

47 International Festival of Highland Folklore in Zakopane 2015. (Aug 28, 2015).
   https://bit.ly/33xYMlE
Le Mystere des Voix Bulgares – Full Performance (Live on KEXP). (Jun 27, 2017).
   https://bit.ly/2Mhzpz5
Rustavi Choir (Georgian Polyphony) Channel.
   https://bit.ly/2OWkoFa
Zedashe (Georgian Folk Group) YouTube Channel.
   https://bit.ly/2Z6rTZU

Convenient links to online resources listed here are also available at GIA Publications website. Visit www.giamusic.com/firststepsglobal.

Alphabetical Listing of Songs

First Steps Categorical Listing of Songs

About the Author

Karen Howard is Associate Professor of Music at the University of St. Thomas in Minnesota. She was an elementary music teacher for many years, and also directed an early childhood music and movement program. She teaches undergraduate and graduate courses in music education, vocal music, and global music, and oversees graduate music research. She is a national and international clinician, presenting on topics ranging from matters of diversity, vocal traditions, children's music culture, and folkloric dance. Her publications include articles and books related to diversifying repertoire and pedagogical practices in school and university music courses. She is the editor of the newly formed series World Music Initiative, a line dedicated to helping music educators grow their confidence in bringing a wider range of music cultures to their students of all ages.